DISCIPLINE STRATEGY

DISCIPLINE STRATEGY®
A Guide To Making a Great Decision, Becoming Your Own Guru,
and Accomplishing Your Goal

For information contact: Timothy L. Coomer, Ph.D.
http://www.DISCIPLINESTRATEGY.com

10 9 8 7 6 5 4 3 2 1

Published by Forefront Books.

Cover Design by Bruce Gore, Gore Studio Inc.
Interior Design by Bill Kersey, KerseyGraphics
Interior Graphics / Art Credit: Kelly C. Danko

ISBN: 9781948677271 print
ISBN: 9781948677288 e-book

DISCIPLINE STRATEGY

A GUIDE TO

Making a Great Decision, Becoming Your Own GURU,

and Accomplishing Your Goal

TIMOTHY L. COOMER, Ph.D.

CONTENTS

Phase 3

PERFECT AND INTENSIFY YOUR EFFORTS

Phase 4

CELEBRATE AND NURTURE CONTINUOUS GROWTH AND WELL-BEING

INTRODUCTION

"Discipline is the bridge between goals and accomplishment."
—JIM ROHN

When I was a young adult, my mom would often say, "Tim, I think you have your life planned out in a spreadsheet." Guilty as charged! I was a researcher, planner, and hard worker. Overly analytical, detail-oriented, and extremely Type A, I consumed books in search of the secrets to success in health, wealth, parenting, and life. But, at age twenty-one, something happened to balance my imbalances: I married a poet, athlete, and artist.

Sandy is driven more by passion and determination than planning, a trait that makes her the perfect antidote to my logical/analytical personality. Combining these different world views, which at times created some entertaining communication challenges, sharpened our abilities to make decisions, choose significant goals, and accomplish positive life change. A shared philosophy, backed by solid principles, emerged.

In May 2016, I had a medical emergency that almost killed me. I was saved by a surgeon's bold decision to perform an exploratory surgery in the middle of the night. It was one of those defining moments that changes the course of your life and sets new priorities. For me, a surprising new priority emerged—to capture the process for achievement that Sandy and I had unintentionally crafted over the course of thirty years and share it with others.

This book is the result of my experiences as a researcher on life performance and as a serial entrepreneur and on Sandy's experience as a writer, social entrepreneur, and All-World Ironman triathlete. I have always relied heavily on books to guide me through business startups, health issues, raising children, understanding relationships, flying airplanes, and earning a Ph.D. These resources have been essential to my learning, but I often felt they were incomplete, leaving out a key piece of information that I needed to put their principles into action. For example, when our four kids were young, the parenting books suggested using a *time out* to interrupt children's bad choices and teach them that their actions had consequences. That's a great tip, but it didn't go far enough. The books didn't address what to do when your three-year-old goes to his room for time out, lies down on his back in front of the bedroom door, and starts kicking it with all his might!

Business books often suffer from the same problem. Many contain great advice but don't get into what to do when things don't go exactly according to the plan. Guides to weight loss, fighting heart disease, or completing an Ironman usually fail to cover those instances when the weight loss just isn't happening despite your best efforts, when the statin drug the doctors claim will help you beat heart disease actually makes you sick, or when swimming in open water scares the heck out of you. What do you do in these instances?

I believe we need more than yet another simple to-do book, and we certainly don't need another one of the slick, shallow, inspirational, you-can-do-it, pep-rally books that abound in pop culture today. A better approach is to learn a process or system that supports genuine change in any situation and allows you to become your own customized expert. In this way, you will become equipped to:

- Make sound decisions.
- Investigate relevant topics.
- Sort through information with a critical eye.
- Conceive a detailed plan.
- Implement the plan.
- Move forward with passion and perseverance.
- Use logic to evaluate your progress and make adjustments where needed.
- Intensify your efforts where appropriate.
- Take notice of what you have accomplished.
- Enjoy the fruits of your labors.

This process is the DISCIPLINE STRATEGY, and it is your roadmap for change.

HOW TO USE THIS BOOK

Jim Rohn, an author and motivational speaker, once said, "Discipline is the bridge between goals and accomplishment." I've long been fascinated by this powerful statement. I memorized it and even plastered it across my office wall. Now I understand the reason for my fascination: I wanted to understand what discipline really meant. After years of research and experimentation, I now feel confident that I understand this bridge between goals and accomplishment, and I want to share with you what I've discovered. DISCIPLINE STRATEGY is a process you can learn and use to take control of your life, take responsibility for your future, and create long-lasting change.

When I started writing this book, I had four important goals:

1. Write a book that anyone can use to dramatically improve their decision-making and implementation processes.
2. Keep it brief and easy to use—no more than thirty information-packed pages per chapter.
3. Provide worksheets to help you implement what is taught in the DISCIPLINE STRATEGY.

4. Create an online community (www.DISCIPLINESTRATEGY. com) where readers can continue sharing information and ideas with one another.

This book teaches you how to go from the point of decision to the point of life change and life mastery. You can apply this process to any change you want to make in your life. And the more you use this method, the better you will become at effecting change.

I've tried to keep this book devoid of "filler" material. Instead, each chapter gets to the point quickly and with clarity. To me, writing a book is like what President Woodrow Wilson said about giving a speech: "If I am to speak ten minutes, I need a week for preparation; if fifteen minutes, three days; if half an hour, two days; if an hour, I am ready now." I've put the effort into this book to make sure it is as condensed and efficient for you to read as possible. I don't like fluff, and you won't find any in this book.

I encourage you to read through the whole book quickly to get a feel for the process. Then go back through it slowly, using each chapter and the additional online worksheets mentioned throughout the book as a guide to walk you through the change process. You'll find additional commentary and guidance on our website and social media. Visit www.DISCIPLINESTRATEGY.com for information on everything we have online. So, get at it, learn from it, and use the DISCIPLINE STRATEGY to set a new course for your life!

OVERVIEW OF THE DISCIPLINE STRATEGY

The DISCIPLINE STRATEGY will empower you to guide your own change initiatives. This system works in personal situations, relationships, businesses, and more. In fact, I have used it to hit new levels of growth in every part of my life. At the heart of the system is the belief that successful change happens at the intersection of intention and strategy. The ten parts of DISCIPLINE STRATEGY, outlined in the following and expanded throughout this book, are based on the DISCIPLINE acronym and broken into four phases:

Phase 1: *Choosing the Destination and Preparing for the Journey*
D – Decide
I – Investigate
S – Sort

Phase 2: *Create the Roadmap and Begin the Journey*
C – Conceive
I – Implement
P – Persevere

Phase 3: *Perfect and Intensify your Efforts*
L – Loop
I – Intensify

Phase 4: *Celebrate and Nurture Continuous Growth and Well-being*
N – Notice
E – Enjoy

Each chapter will thoroughly explore one of these ten steps of the DISCIPLINE STRATEGY process.

CHAPTER 1: DECIDE

A decision is the first step in applying the DISCIPLINE STRATEGY. In the business world, considerable thought, discussion, and research go into important decisions. In our personal lives, we sometimes make a commitment to change after experiencing an intensely emotional moment. Perhaps, after years of personal struggle, we decide it is time to confront a hard issue and make a willful decision to change something. Or, if you're like me, you might use goal-setting to get to the decision point. No matter how you come to that important moment, every change—whether in your personal life, career, business, or any other facet of life—starts with a decision.

The word *decision* comes from the Latin word *decidere*, which means "to cut off." That's exactly what a decision does—it cuts off all other possibilities. It is an *inflection point* in life. A decision is not a wish or a dream; it's the most powerful thing a human being can do because it involves redirecting the entire course of one's life.

Decision-making is fraught with challenges, however. Therefore, before we can build the entire DISCIPLINE STRATEGY, we must first lay the foundation by understanding how decisions are best made and how decision-making can go wrong. In Chapter 1 you will learn how to better understand the decision-making process, evaluate your many choices, and select the path that is best for you.

CHAPTER 2: INVESTIGATE

Once a decision has been made, you must investigate and do research so that you can make a plan based on solid facts. This task may seem easier than ever now in the Information Age, but the Internet is filled with misinformation—some of it simply wrong and some of it outright dangerous. Knowing how to find trusted sources and go beyond the typical Google search will dramatically improve your ability to gather useful information.

Your investigation process also includes talking with people who are doing what you want to do. One-on-one personal discussions with people who have already walked the path you are about to travel will give you some of your most valuable insights. People love to share their success stories and help others avoid the traps they encountered. You will learn how to reach out to people in a way that encourages them to help you.

One of the most valuable skills I learned as a doctoral student was how to carry out research—locating, evaluating, and sometimes questioning existing knowledge. This chapter will give you a short course on how to think like an expert researcher and find things that other people usually don't find. We will walk through some specific examples of how investigations can go wrong and how to avoid typical mistakes. You will emerge from this chapter with new skills, confidence, and purpose as a researcher.

CHAPTER 3: SORT

Once you complete your investigation, you'll probably have a rather large pile of information. While some filtering should occur during the investigation process (chapter 2), you will still have to determine what is relevant and useful to you. In this chapter, we will focus on how to sort through the mounds of research and select the material that will help you conceive a plan with the highest probability of success.

Rather than blindly trusting the first page of results from a Google search, you will learn a more scientific sorting method you can apply to your research that will help you judge the material's truthfulness and acceptance by people "in the know." You will also learn how to summarize and digest this information so you will be ready to conceive a plan.

CHAPTER 4: CONCEIVE

Your decision will ultimately lead you to a new destination. Getting to that point and realizing your vision will require a well-conceived plan. Think about what it takes to build a large skyscraper or an aircraft carrier, each of which could have nearly one billion parts. *Someone* has figured out how to think through and manage every detail of these complex plans. We can learn from them and simplify the science to serve our needs. As the late British prime minister Margaret Thatcher said, "Plan your work for today and every day, then work your plan."

The process of conceiving a plan is often underrated or skipped altogether, but the time you spend planning is some of the best time you will invest in this whole process. Plus, conceiving a plan has a deeper and broader meaning than you might expect. The word *conceive* comes from the Latin word *concipere*, or "to take fully; take in." So part of conceiving the plan involves taking it into your mind, your subconscious, and your soul. You will learn how to make the plan part of your being so that every aspect of your mind is searching for answers and working on the plan twenty-four hours a day. I'll also teach you about the reticular activation system in your brain, which will support your plan if you train it appropriately. This is not hocus pocus; this is leveraging the science of how your brain works for your benefit.

Yes, you will conceive a plan, but—more importantly—you will integrate the plan into every fiber of your mental, physical, and spiritual self.

CHAPTER 5: IMPLEMENT

Implementing a plan is a distinctly different endeavor from conceiving a plan. I have seen some great plans conceived, documented, and hailed as the beginning of a remarkable success story—only to collapse because no thought was given to their implementation. Implementation is about habits, priorities, and understanding the real challenges involved: setbacks, roadblocks, new developments, and wandering focus. Implementing a plan has a scientific component to it, just like conceiving a plan, but it is also an art that entails a deep understanding of human psychology. When we are planning, we are usually enjoying the dopamine high and excitement associated with envisioning our success; however, when we actually start *implementing* the plan, we come face-to-face with our demons. In Christopher Columbus's time, maps marked unexplored waters with the words, "Here be dragons." As you go about implementing your plan and venturing into unexplored areas of thought, you will confront dragons too. Don't worry, though; we will discuss how to turn these terrifying dragons into cowering dogs.

CHAPTER 6: PERSEVERE

Think basic talent is the key to success? Think again. Recent research shows that talent is actually overrated. Instead, passion, perseverance, and a positive outlook are the keys to personal growth and accomplishment. These things make up *grit*, a relatively new concept that has received considerable attention from both academic researchers and leadership experts. If you truly want to win, you've got to understand how to cultivate and maximize grit.

In this context, we will also probe the concept of psychological capital or PsyCap, which encompasses Hope, Efficacy, Resiliency, and Optimism—or your HERO within. Progress in the face of obstacles comes from passion, perseverance, and a high level of PsyCap. You will learn how to nurture these character traits, discover your HERO, and apply the tools of positive psychology to fuel your progress.

CHAPTER 7: LOOP

One of the more difficult steps in the DISCIPLINE STRATEGY process is the loop step. At this point, it is necessary to take a sober look at what is working and where the struggles are. This requires a rather high level of pragmatic thinking. You need to understand logically what you are not doing well and where you need to improve. These findings may require you to loop back to previous steps and make adjustments. The challenge here is to figure out when you need to dig deep and show the grit needed to press forward with your established plan and, if necessary, to make changes. I'll give you a plan for doing this while also helping you avoid the traps of self-doubt and regret that often come with self-examination. You will also learn how to critically self-assess and benchmark your progress against independent outside sources.

CHAPTER 8: INTENSIFY

After tweaking your plan through the loop process, you'll be ready to intensify your efforts, like a race car driver flooring it down the straightaway. By this point, you'll have determined what works and you'll know exactly where you're headed. You'll also have tested, researched, and implemented various approaches, techniques, and habits. It is now time to focus with laserlike intensity on pushing hard toward your goal.

CHAPTER 9: NOTICE

Everything in life eventually goes back to normal—or at least settles into a *new* normal. People who win big in the lottery soon return, in most cases, to their pre-lottery level of happiness and, believe it or not, their pre-lottery net worth. On the other hand, people who become paralyzed due to a traumatic injury are typically back to their pre-accident level of happiness within a couple years. I have suffered a near-death experience myself and can testify that it is an effective way to adjust your mindset so that you more fully notice and appreciate your daily blessings. However, you have to nurture that awareness to maintain it over time.

Once you are well on your way to achieving your goal, you must take notice of what is different. Create a habit of expressing gratitude for the changes you have made and are continuing to make. Do not let your accomplishments fade too quickly into the abyss of normalization. Your self-confidence, sometimes called self-efficacy and an important byproduct of the DISCIPLINE

STRATEGY, will be nurtured if you stop and notice the obstacles you have surmounted and the person you have become. As Jim Rohn once said, "The ultimate reason for setting goals is to entice you to become the person it takes to achieve them."

CHAPTER 10: ENJOY

Finally, at the end of the process, you must make time to *enjoy* your accomplishment! Celebrate with friends and mark the success of your journey with remembrances of your achievement. This celebration will look different for everyone based on each one's unique personality, but, regardless of your nature, you can consciously choose to experience a sense of satisfaction. We will look at some specific strategies for enjoying what you have accomplished and avoid what I call the "Is this all there is?" mentality.

ABOUT THE STORIES AND PEOPLE YOU WILL MEET

In many chapters, I'll use composite stories based on real people I've known or read about during the last thirty-five years. These stories focus on specific challenges and contain some fictionalized circumstances and settings. The primary reason for using composite stories is to protect people's privacy and avoid embarrassing anyone. After all, no one wants to be the poster boy or girl for how to do something wrong! The names have been changed, but the situations are real.

This book is scientifically based, personally inspirational, and educationally entertaining. The principles are essential, but the stories make them come to life and should both inspire you and enable you to apply the DISCIPLINE STRATEGY to your own personal situation.

We have quite a journey ahead, and it all starts with a decision. It's time to cut off other options and get to work on a process that will change how you approach your work, relationships, and life.

Let's get started.

PHASE

1

CHOOSING THE DESTINATION
AND PREPARING FOR
THE JOURNEY

CHAPTER 1

DECIDE

"It is in your moments of decision that your destiny is shaped."
—Tony Robbins

The power of a decision cannot be underestimated. As I mentioned in the Introduction, the Latin root word for "decision," *decidere*, literally means "to cut off." So when you make a decision, you cut off all other paths. Making a decision is not wishing that something will happen or thinking that maybe it will happen; it means taking action to *cause* something to happen. It is one of the most powerful things we can do to change ourselves and our future.

Our capacity for conscious evaluation and decision is one of the many things that distinguishes humans from other mammals. But our decision-making process is driven by a brain that has evolved from a very different context, with different environmental conditions and threats. As a result, the decisions we make often leave us unfulfilled. Because the journey into the DISCIPLINE STRATEGY begins at the point of decision, you must understand the power and pitfalls of decision-making.

THE GROUND-LEVEL VIEW
(WHAT THIS LOOKS LIKE IN REAL LIFE)

Bobby had chased a dream, based on a decision made many years before, to become a high-powered corporate lawyer. He had worked hard to get into one of the nation's best law schools, and he fought to get the right internships and to impress his prospective employer's partners. The result was the fulfillment of Bobby's dream—a job as a junior associate at one of Atlanta's largest law firms. Now, just six months into this fabulous dream career, Bobby was miserable. He was working seventy-plus hours per week, leaving him with little time for his girlfriend, Rhonda. He was getting out of shape physically and was on a downward mental slide. At 3:00 a.m. one sleepless night, tossing and turning in bed, he asked himself, *What went wrong?*

Bobby's story is common. Many of the decisions we make are based on an attempt to project ourselves into the future and into a situation we know very little about. Bobby was a twenty-year-old undergraduate at the University of Tennessee when he formed his vision of being a corporate lawyer and made a major life decision to pursue the path of law school, choice internships, and a coveted slot at a big law firm. Now at age twenty-six, Bobby is $175,000 in debt (mostly school loans), single (Rhonda found better options), and still wondering what went wrong.

On the other side of the country is Phil, age sixty-one, a retired production supervisor from a mid-sized manufacturing company just outside Portland, Oregon. The plant where he worked for over forty years is not far from the beautiful Columbia River that separates Oregon from Washington state. Phil married his sweetheart, Elisabeth, right out of high school and started working at the plant—the only one job he had his entire adult life. He and Elisabeth raised three children, the youngest of whom has just turned thirty, who have settled into their own life journeys. An avid fisherman, Phil had eagerly planned and waited for retirement, when he would have plenty of time to spend on the nearby

Columbia River. Phil had often found himself, when working long production shifts at the plant, dreaming about relaxing afternoons on the river with his custom rod and reel. Now, eighteen months into his *dream* retirement, Phil is depressed, confused, and feeling more stress in his marriage than at any time during their forty-two years together. Fishing just doesn't seem that interesting to him anymore, and he is wondering what is going on, why he feels so lost, and what to do about it.

These stories illustrate the challenges we all face when making decisions that affect our future. Our decisions often lead us into situations and circumstances we did not foresee and that create considerable stress. A better understanding of the science of decision-making along with specific strategies to circumvent the pitfalls will help you make better decisions and lay the ground-work for the next step in the DISCIPLINE STRATEGY.

THE CHALLENGES AND SOLUTIONS

Evolutionary forces have not yet optimized our decision-making processes for the modern age. We still tend to make decisions through a process that relies heavily on quick judgment and the fight-or-flight response—impulses that lead to a lot of missteps and challenges. Fortunately, research has done an excellent job of identifying the pitfalls and illuminating effective strategies to help us become aware of, understand, and avoid the biggest traps.

Let's start by taking a look at the five biggest challenges of decision-making. You will notice that several of these strategies are intertwined. To help you remember these dangers, we will use the acronym POWER:

- **LIMITED PERSPECTIVE:** You must understand your perspective on the problem or decision and realize that it may be limited and thereby limit your possibilities.
- **LIMITED OPTIONS:** You may be limiting yourself with regard to perceived options. This occurs when our built-in mental governor filters our thoughts and is blind to other realistic

options. You may also simply not be gathering and nurturing options that are available to you.

- **WEB OF DECEIT:** Our brains create an amazing web of deceit that is typically invisible to us. You can think of this as that little voice in your head that tells you what you *can't* do and why you will fail, self-defeating messages that create a steady stream of negative self-talk. We have to shine a light on this web of deceit and become aware of how it influences our thinking and decision-making.

- **EMOTIONALITY:** It is critical to move out of your emotional self, engage your brain, and put yourself into your most logical mind. Operating on emotions is like flying an airplane through a cloudy mountain range guided only by your "gut" feeling—it won't work and the outcome will likely be disastrous.

- **RESISTING REROUTE:** Before you even begin to put together an action plan to turn your decision into reality, you must anticipate that a lot of rerouting will occur before you reach your final destination.

Now that you've seen the big picture of these five pitfalls, let's zoom in and take a much closer look at each one, detailing the problem and outlining the best solutions as we go.

CHALLENGE: LIMITED PERSPECTIVE

When I was about ten years old, I had a good friend who lived a couple streets over. We were inseparable as kids, exploring our neighborhood pond and riding our bikes across what we saw as vast, boundless landscapes (but what was really about ten city blocks). As we grew older, we became more adventurous. One day, we decided to see just how high we could climb up a tree in my friend's back yard. Would we be able to see over the hills around our neighborhood and get a glance of the Nashville skyline just five miles away? The idea was both thrilling and terrifying to my ten-year-old mind. So, I climbed. As I moved up the tree, I noticed a dramatic change in perspective. First, I could look down on some of the cars in nearby driveways. Next, I could see the roofs of the surrounding houses. Finally, as I reached a point where no ten-year-old boy should have been, I saw Nashville's gleaming skyline and skyscrapers. From that new vantage point, I had a clearer sense of where I was and how everything in my little world fit together. I could see my elementary school, the pond where we played, the downtown area, and my own home a few blocks away. The whole world looked very different.

This kind of top-level, broad perspective is the place where your decision-making process must start. If you're facing a possible career change, for example, you can't start by asking yourself, *Should I quit my job or not?* That's far too narrow; you will definitely not make an optimized decision. Instead, start with a higher perspective and ask a series of questions:

- Are there changes I can make in my job that would increase my satisfaction with it?
- Is my job the problem, or is there some deep dissatisfaction within myself that I need to address?
- What are the things I was passionate about years ago, and are there ways to pursue those things with renewed interest and vigor?

Those are simple examples, but there are dozens of questions you could ask yourself in this situation. The point is to broaden your perspective, to climb the tree that lets you see all the options, and to survey the landscape. This is where you should begin.

SOLUTION: EXPAND YOUR PERSPECTIVE

The solution to a limited perspective, from which we all suffer, is to expand it by applying several specific strategies.

TALK WITH TRUSTED FRIENDS AND ADVISORS

A close friend, sibling, spouse, parent, child, coworker, counselor, or minister sees you differently from how you see yourself. You must be willing to seek real, honest feedback from the people who know you best. Develop a list of questions and tell your friends you are implementing some techniques you learned by reading about the DISCIPLINE STRATEGY and want their feedback. You'll see information at the end of this chapter about a worksheet I've created for this purpose.

USE PSYCHOMETRICS

Psychometrics are scientifically tested and validated tests of your personality and aptitude. These tests can tell you a surprising amount about yourself and your personality, interests, abilities, and communication style. The MyPersonality® assessment is designed to accompany this book (learn more at www.DISCIPLINESTRATEGY.com). When you take the assessment, you will receive a detailed report that will help you expand your perspective and better execute the DISCIPLINE STRATEGY process. I'll provide more information about how to access the MyPersonality assessment at the end of this chapter.

KEEP A JOURNAL

One way to tap into your subconscious and make it part of your conscious thinking and perspective is to journal. This requires setting aside time each day to write. Your journal entries should be unfiltered and should capture your greatest aspirations and fears.

GET MORE EXPERIENCE

What can you do to get a better idea of what this decision will actually look like in your life? For example, suppose you have decided to become a professional pilot. Before quitting your job and going to one of those year-long, intensive flight-training courses, you should probably talk to some pilots and hear what their lives are really like. You should also get your private pilot license and do some flying to see how it feels to be in command of an aircraft on your own. As you progress and earn more licenses, you might even see if you could fly as a copilot a few times and learn from a commercial charter pilot. Or say you have decided to become a full-time yoga instructor. You could start by getting the first couple of certifications and teaching at night and on weekends. The point is to take small steps to get real-life experience related to the decision you are making. This real-life experience prevents you from imagining only a glowing, idyllic view of this future life. Perhaps you'll learn from the commercial charter pilot that he is spending twenty nights a month away from home and feels that it is a difficult life for his family that includes two young children. Or maybe a full-time yoga instructor will tell you that her lifestyle is even better than she ever dreamed because of the new level of fitness, peace, friendships, and life balance she has achieved.

Whatever decision you're facing, find some way to bring the reality of the decision into your world. Real-life experience—good and bad—is simply irreplaceable.

TRAVEL

Your day-to-day routines can support your decisions and goals, but they can also smother your perspective. Travel allows you to move away from daily routines, obligations, and technology and opens you up to new ideas and ways of thinking.

Some of my best decisions, for whatever reason, have been made while I was standing beside large bodies of water. I have made pivotal decisions while on a cliff in Nova Scotia looking out over the North Atlantic, while skipping rocks on the Talkeetna River in Alaska, and while watching the sun set on Seven Mile Beach in the Cayman Islands. Perhaps what works for you is a walk down a wooded trail in the mountains. Or maybe it is the exciting atmosphere of a British Premier League soccer game. Whatever you love to do, wherever you love to go, go there and give your mind the freedom to explore. Then *think*. Open your mind to the larger world around you, take off your blinders, set aside the rules that govern your daily life, and open yourself to the incredible possibilities. What can you do? Where can you go? How big will you dream today?

COUNSELING

A wise man once said, "We all have some crap to deal with." As a result, counseling can be a route to a new and broader perspective. If you have been struggling with a specific topic for an extended period of time, you may need some help breaking through and changing your perspective. Counseling is a tool that anyone can access. It should not have any stigma, and it can be a powerfully worthwhile process.

CHALLENGE: LIMITED OPTIONS

We all tend to filter our thoughts and dreams because of limiting beliefs. Sometimes this controlling governor on our thought processes is so effective that we don't realize we have eliminated options before they were even considered. To counter this, you need to compose a robust list of all your options. As you move to the right perspective, new options will emerge into your field of view. I like to call this *unfiltered brainstorming*, a time when you can put everything on the table and keep all your options open. *Unfiltered* means you write down every single thing that comes to mind without weeding anything out. If you think, *I could move to Italy and teach English to grade-school kids*, then that goes on the list of possibilities.

Also, realize that the decisions you make will affect your subsequent options down the road. You always want to create options and keep them in your back pocket. You want to collect options as if they were fine gems, harvesting and nurturing them, never taking one off the table until you have given it full consideration. Even then, file that option in the top drawer so you know exactly where it is should you decide to come back for it later.

SOLUTION: EXPAND YOUR OPTIONS

Expanding your options is part mind game and part shift in life strategy. There is a subtle but distinct difference between changing your perspective and expanding your options. Perspective has to do with how you *view* your situation; options have to do with what you might *do* in your situation. So if you're asking, *Should I quit my job?* a new perspective might change the question into, *What could I pursue in my life with passion and intensity?* When you look for options to apply to that new perspective, you'll open up a whole new world of possibilities. Here are some specific strategies you can utilize to expand your options.

UNFILTERED BRAINSTORMING

I've already mentioned this strategy, but here I will suggest a specific method for doing it. First, ask one or two (but no more than two) friends or family members to join you for a few hours of brainstorming. Pick these people carefully; they need to know you well, but they must not be limiting factors in your life (i.e., don't pick a naysayer). Second, get away from your usual environment. Don't do this at home or at your office. Instead, find a neutral or inspiring space—a room at the local library, a table in a nearby park, or a beautiful vacation spot. Take a large, sticky-note easel pad and some markers with you. Explain to your helpers what you are trying to do: "Our goal today is to create an unfiltered list of options for my next _____." Perhaps you are working on your next career move, solving a weight or health issue, becoming a better salesperson, or any of the hundreds of life scenarios we all experience. Your friends will help you generate a wider range of ideas than you alone could ever think of. Every single thought should be recorded on the pad. Remember, this is *unfiltered* brainstorming.

REVISIT PREVIOUS PASSIONS

Another way to expand your options is to recall your previous passions. What did you give up in the past due to insecurities, missed opportunities, youthful poor judgment, financial concerns, or some other obstacle? Identifying these and being open to explore them once again may identify new paths to accomplish them or move them into focus as a renewed goal.

When I was in my twenties, for example, I wanted to get a Ph.D. in business. However, that seemed like an impossible dream back then when I was working on a master's degree and I was already married with our first child on the way. As I got older and life got even more complicated, it always seemed too difficult to figure out how to reach that goal. But something changed when I turned fifty. A few things aligned, including an unexpected life change, the sale of my business, and the emergence of a newly designed Ph.D. program for executives. With a renewed passion for doctoral education, I embarked on the journey I never thought would be possible and completed my Ph.D.—thirty years after first nursing that dream. That only happened because I never lost sight of a passion I had when I was younger and because I kept evaluating, every few years, the feasibility of that goal.

Never write something off simply because it seems too hard or too outlandish at this point in your life. The world is a dynamic place, and what looks impossible today just might be possible in the years ahead. In the words of the great Yogi Berra, "It ain't over till it's over."

BE A LIFETIME LEARNER
My wise father once said, "Everything you learn is of value." The wisdom in that statement has been proven over and over throughout my life. Do not become stagnant. Strive continuously to learn, grow, and expand your knowledge, experience, and capabilities. This keeps your set of options growing and allows you to combine knowledge from multiple arenas to create unique ideas.

Becoming a lifetime learner is incredibly easy in today's world. The only barrier between you and learning *anything* is your desire, passion, and commitment. Some specific strategies for lifetime learning include:

1. Listen to audiobooks while walking and driving. You can buy them individually, subscribe to a membership service such as Audible (www.audible.com), or even check them out free from your public library's website.
2. Commit to reading. Library books, e-books, and online material are all readily available and affordable. Pick your topics of interest and read, read, read! Replacing just thirty minutes a day of useless TV time with reading can expand your options exponentially.
3. Take advantage of free online courses. Check out www.coursera.org, for example. This amazing organization offers an unbelievable array of learning opportunities, mostly for free, from top universities. You will be amazed at what you can learn through these courses. You should also visit Khan Academy, a free online learning resource.
4. Consider investing in the Great Courses organization (www.thegreatcoursesplus.com), which offers courses on a broad variety of topics. For the cost of one restaurant meal per month, you could have access to an unbelievable volume of quality education.
5. Explore the resources available on Google Scholar. A lot of the best university-level research sits behind a paywall, but you can usually at least access summaries and abstracts of research articles on any topic you can imagine.

Commit to being a lifetime learner. Start now and you'll be amazed at how your brain will begin to generate new ideas, passions, interests, and options for your life.

IDENTIFY AND DESTROY FEAR
I like to laugh at fear. Remember, the human brain has evolved to protect us; it doesn't want you to accidentally stumble across a saber tooth tiger and become his lunch. Your brain has a fight-or-flight response mechanism it invokes when it confronts strange places, unusual circumstances, or perceived danger—but much of

the fear you feel isn't justified. During a decision-making process, fear is often the result of worrying about making a *wrong* decision. Or fear arises when we start trying to project ourselves into a future situation.

First, realize there is not necessarily one *right* decision. There are so many paths to pursue in life. Make a decision based on the best thought process possible; then, commit to that path and work to improve it as you go along. The truth is, you will *never* make a perfect decision. Observe the fear you are feeling, but do not let it limit your options. Set the fear aside and know that it will subside as the unfamiliarity of your decision decreases and you begin to realize the fruits of your decision. Nothing is typically as bad as we fear. Do you know what I usually find on the other side of my fears? Nothing. The thing I dread is almost never actually there at all. Fear is in our minds. It is an *interpretation* of our world, not a state of *reality*. So don't just ignore fear; destroy it.

CHALLENGE: THE WEB OF DECEIT

Our brains have evolved to help us protect ourselves *from* ourselves. The brain defines our universe, gives us rules to live by, and constantly speaks to our minds. But this protector often presents us with a false view of reality. Let's tap into a few brains and hear what the so-called protector has to say:

"She doesn't like you because you don't make enough money."

"Why are you so stupid? Remember, your third grade teacher said you were stupid, and you *did* flunk a civics exam in the fourth grade."

"Your boss really likes Mary more than you. You probably ticked him off when you challenged him the other day in that meeting."

"I don't know why you set goals each year. You always fail, and it just makes you more miserable. Why don't we go out for some pizza and beer and forget all this decision-making garbage? It won't matter anyway."

This web of deceit includes all self-doubt, self-limiting beliefs, negative self-talk, and multiple replays of past failures. Learning to recognize this inner voice and developing strategies to silence it will open a clearer pathway to better decision-making. Here is how you can do it.

SOLUTION: SILENCE THE INNER VOICE

To silence your inner voice, you must first recognize that it exists. We have all become so comfortable with a constant mental dialogue that we begin to think of it as a wise voice we should listen to. The most effective strategy for silencing the mind is awareness and meditation. I recommend Michael Singer's book *The Untethered Soul* as a guide to gaining a deep awareness of how this inner voice can lead you astray. I also recommend the app Headspace for those who want to make a serious effort at meditating. The following couple of paragraphs will give you a short course on this topic, but if you think this is a real problem for you, I encourage you to explore my recommended resources.

Let's give meditation a try right now. Close your eyes for about five minutes and simply listen to your thoughts. Then, come back to this page. Seriously, close your eyes and listen. Don't read ahead without doing this right now.

Now, what did you hear? How quickly did your mind take over and ramble through a maze of thoughts, worries, and future planning? Were your thoughts useful? Did they create anxiety? Were they filled with positivity, or did they lean more toward negative thoughts? The greatest source of anxiety is our own mind as we ruminate on the past and attempt to predict the future. Both are typically wastes of time. Increase your awareness of the mental dialogue and challenge it. Laugh when an old tape runs through your mind and see it for the useless rerun that it is. Consciously choose to replace repetitive or negative thoughts with new, positive imagery and a focus on gratitude. This is a mental muscle that you can build through conscious effort, and awareness is the first step.

I always considered myself a pretty even-tempered, logical, calm guy—that is, until I started working with the Headspace app and realized just how scattered and uncontrolled my mind was. During the simple exercises of sitting silently and being aware of my own breathing, I would drift off mentally after about ten seconds! As the app teaches, once I realized my mind had wandered, I would gently guide it back to the present. Over time, my awareness slowly branched out from this daily ten-minute exercise to times during the day when I would consciously decide to stop my mental gyrations and bring my mind into the present. Meditation is a learned skill that benefits your daily life far beyond the specific times when you are meditating. In fact, the benefit I have found most important is my newly trained ability to choose to control my thoughts.

Understanding the web of deceit and the voices in your head, in combination with meditation, will dramatically improve your decision-making because you will sidestep the web that entangles your every waking thought and trips you up with doubt and insecurity.

CHALLENGE: EMOTIONALITY

I am an early riser, typically waking at 4:45 a.m. I love to get up and exercise for about an hour, then shower and head to work where I put on a big pot of coffee. However, I hate to admit that my first thought in the morning, somewhere around 4:46 a.m., is often a negative one. I don't know why this is, but I know if I made decisions based on my thinking process at 4:46 a.m., I would end up sleeping until 9:00 a.m. and spend the rest of the day sitting on the couch watching YouTube videos and eating Nutella straight from the jar. That is exactly why I don't design my life at 4:46 a.m.! Instead, I jumpstart my brain with my morning routine of writing in my gratitude journal, exercising, meditating, and then *boom!* I am in my right mind and feel invincible.

You need to learn how to engage your brain on a daily basis and know, with confidence, that the doubts and negative emotional mindset can be overcome every day through good habits. You will not make it far if you struggle with emotion, doubt, and the highs and lows of the randomness typical of an undisciplined life. You need to engage your best mind, the unemotional and optimistic mind, each day before you make decisions.

SOLUTION: ENGAGE YOUR BRAIN

Emotion-based thinking emerges when we are tired, sick, weak, hungry, stressed, afraid, vulnerable, angry, or insecure. To avoid emotion-based decision-making, you first need to be aware of when you are working from emotionality and decide not to make a decision while in that state.

It took us a few years, but Sandy and I decided at some point in our marriage that there would be no heavy conversations after 8:00 p.m. Evening conversations never turned out well because we were typically both exhausted from dealing with children, work, exercise, and life events. After 8:00 p.m., it was less likely that our brains would be operating in a logical manner. You need to find and understand your own limits. Going back to the example of my morning regimen, I don't decide at 4:45 a.m. whether I am going to get up and work out. That decision was made a long time ago.

I encourage you to determine how you get into your best frame of mind. You are at your best when you are rested, mentally at peace, focused, and in an optimistic mindset. I have found my own path to this place, and it is when I am there that I make decisions. You need to find your path to the state of logical rather than emotion-driven thinking and make your decisions from that vantage point.

My pattern is to complete my morning routine, meditate, then close my office door, put on a musical playlist, and stand in front of a large wall painted with whiteboard paint where I can sketch out my plans. These plans come from my best mind and are written on the wall that faces my desk. I am reminded of these plans constantly during the day, and when I find my mind drifting back into emotional thinking (I will spare you the details of my internal dialogue), I can lift my eyes from my computer and see in my own handwriting what path I have decided to follow.

Find your path to your best mind and chart your course when you are in that condition. Write it down where you can see it and reinforce your decision. Then you can reassure yourself later, "I already made the decision when I was most wise, rested, and logical. I will not debate this now. I just have to do it."

CHALLENGE: RESISTING REROUTE

As a mechanical engineering student many years ago, I was fascinated with materials science. I had not been exposed to the subject previously, and some of its details amazed me. One particular concept that has remained with me over the years is the relationship between strength and brittleness. I had thought these two conditions were opposites but, in fact, a very strong material can also be brittle. The idea of being both strong and flexible is an exciting area of materials science research today, and it provides a great analogy for how we should view our decisions.

A decision, once made, cannot be inflexible and closed to revision. Obstacles may require you to change your route. When I learned to fly a plane, I was taught that, when flying between two cities, you are rarely precisely on course. Instead, you must make constant, minor course corrections that keep you *close* to your course. You remain aware of where you are heading and adjust. Occasionally, due to weather, you have to make major course corrections. Sometimes you even have to change your final destination. As a pilot, you don't just *plan* for the deviations—you *expect* them. You don't give up and return home; you reroute and continue your journey.

Staying aware of the potential need to reroute is important in helping you manage expectations. If you decide, *I am going to get a job in Italy this summer*, but then you run into an unexpected ban on temporary immigrant jobs in Italy, you don't need to give up. You have to be open to rerouting.

SOLUTION: PLAN FOR THE ALTERNATIVE

In certain aviation scenarios, when filing a flight plan to fly to another airport, you are required by regulations to have an alternative destination and enough fuel to reach your original destination and then continue on to your alternative destination. This is a perfect analogy for the decision-making process. Acknowledge the possibility that something may go wrong at any point along the way, even when you are within sight of the goal. Include in your plans an alternative place to stop, assess the situation, and devise a new route. Obstacles do not equal failure! But running out of fuel and crashing due to a lack of an alternative—that's a failure you can't walk away from.

Here's how to plan an alternative. First, construct a *premortem*. Before you complete your decision-making process, imagine scenarios in which you fail. Some success gurus will tell you to never think a negative thought, but research shows that if you imagine on the front end all the things that could go wrong, you will have a much greater probability of success. Anticipating possible failure allows you to anticipate a path around the causes of failure. Understanding the potential challenges will also help you be more alert to mounting obstacles.

Then file your flight plan, metaphorically speaking. Lay out within your decision timeline a plan for when you'll reassess possible changes. When a pilot implements a flight plan, he knows where he expects to be at any given time along the way. If his actual location doesn't line up with the planned location at a given time, he needs to figure out what the heck is going on. It's the same way with your decision. If you are planning to lose weight and have a "flight plan" to drop from 200 to 180 pounds in three months, but you still weigh 198 after two months, then you need to verify what is going wrong. Don't throw in the towel, but refer to your premortem analysis and perhaps go to Plan B.

DECIDE TO BE A HERO

A simple decision can change the course of your life. You have the power to decide on something different, better, new, exciting, and growth-oriented. You can decide how to solve problems, improve your health, create career opportunities, improve your relationships, and a million other things. It's your choice! I hope this chapter has encouraged you to embrace that truth and make a decision for positive change.

Joseph Campbell, author of *The Power of Myth* and who was the American Professor of Literature at Sarah Lawrence College, is credited with a quote that sums up the power of a decision. He says, "You are the hero of your own life's story." I believe that quote to be true, and I know you have the power to begin your story anew with the power of a decision. This is where it all begins, in the moment of the decision. The chapters ahead are all about training your hero within so that you can reach the point of accomplishment.

———— TAKE IT FURTHER ————

Reading about these principles is great, but *information* alone can only take you so far. To get the most out of *DISCIPLINE STRATEGY*, you need to pair the concepts in this book with the action-oriented *application* resources available at www.DISCIPLINESTRATEGY.com. Head over there right now and download/access the following worksheets and resources that correspond to this chapter.

Perspective Expansion Worksheet
This worksheet will walk you through a process designed to expand your perspective on your life and your decision landscape.

MyPersonality Assessment

As explained in this chapter, psychometric tools use a series of questions to identify personality traits and tendencies. I have designed a customized personality test, MyPersonality, to accompany the DISCIPLINE STRATEGY, and I have made it available to readers of this book at no additional cost. MyPersonality will provide you with new and perhaps critical insights into your personality that you can immediately apply to the DISCIPLINE STRATEGY process. After you complete the assessment, you will receive a personalized report. Take the test for free today at www.DISCIPLINESTRATEGY.com using the code **85285**.

Daily Journal

There are a lot of great daily journals on the market, but we have provided a Daily Journal template aligned with the DISCIPLINE STRATEGY. Print several copies of this worksheet and create your own journal using a three-ring binder.

Unfiltered Brainstorming

This worksheet guides you through the process of a brainstorming session and provides guidelines and prompts to stimulate discussion.

Identifying Previous Passions

Most of us have long forgotten some of the passions of our youth or early adult years. This worksheet helps you rediscover those passions. This can be considered a subcategory of your brainstorming, but it is important enough to deserve its own worksheet.

CHAPTER 2

INVESTIGATE

*"Beware of false knowledge; it is more
dangerous than ignorance."*
—George Bernard Shaw

I wrote my first research paper in 1979 for a high school science fair. The topic was fuel-efficient aircraft design. I loved the topic and went on to win a NASA science award for my work. This positive reinforcement added to my fascination with research.

During the investigative phase of this project, I went to the library, found a copy of what was then called the Thomas Registry (an exhaustive sourcebook on products made by American manufacturers), searched for appropriate articles, tracked down those sources in books or on microfilm, read them, and prepared note cards summarizing my discoveries. On a good day, I would get through perhaps four or five sources using this laborious process. However, I never doubted the authenticity of the information or worried if my sources contained biases or misinformation. Perhaps I should have been a little more skeptical, but the information in these sources was generally solid, even if incomplete. The choices were limited at that time, so the issue of deciding what was the best or most authentic information seldom came up. I simply used what I had.

Things are very different today. I just now did a Google search for "fuel-efficient aircraft design." It took 0.67 seconds to deliver more than 1.5 *million* references to choose from. Switching to Google Scholar, a tool that generally searches scholarly literature, I found 205,000 much more substantive references in 0.08 seconds. Such a wealth of information makes our research and investigative efforts easier than ever, but those millions of search results also bring with them a problem I never had when I first began studying aircraft mechanics.

You see, our incredible access to information today creates a serious dilemma. We can find an unbelievable number of information sources—many of which are inconsistent with one another—and there is no obvious way to determine what is true or most applicable to our investigation. Or to put it another way, we're never sure which sources are reliable and which ones are worthless, incomplete, inconsistent, or downright lies.

In this chapter, "Investigate," I want to address that challenge by outlining a process for investigating a topic and gathering a balanced set of information. Then, the following chapter, "Sort," will walk you through how to sort through the information and select what to use as the foundation for your plan. So how do we learn to be good investigators?

In his books and speeches, the great performance coach and writer Lou Tice frequently refers to the "who-said of the highest authority." He means that we tend to quickly accept information if it comes to us from some perceived authority figure. However, some sources that claim to be authoritative are actually quite unreliable. A good example is the late-night infomercial spokesperson hawking the latest fitness program that will get you "ripped" in only six weeks. Or that testosterone booster you see in the back of sports magazines. Or (one of my favorites), the longstanding ad in *Popular Mechanics* magazine for a small vial of pheromones you can add to your aftershave to "get more affection from women."

It should be fairly easy for us to call these products and marketing pitches out as fakes; they're the grown-up equivalents of the X-ray specs you might have seen advertised in the back of comic books when you were a child. But what about the thousands of other commercials, products, remedies, vendors, schools, institutions, drugs, health habits, books, and informational web pages? How can you do effective investigation and build reliable, actionable knowledge to support you in reaching the goal established during your decision-making process? Let's find out.

THE GROUND-LEVEL VIEW
(WHAT THIS LOOKS LIKE IN REAL LIFE)

In high school, Sam loved watching HGTV. He grew up in Westlake, a suburb just west of Cleveland and a stone's throw from Lake Erie. As he drove to Westlake High School each morning, he would notice what types of homes were selling and what was being built.

After graduating from high school, Sam attended Lorain County Community College while working part-time as a waiter to support himself. Lorain County Community College was great; unlike his buddies at the big state colleges, Sam had built close, personal relationships with his professors and was genuinely enjoying his classes. Overall, he was pretty happy with his decision ... but something was missing. His chosen major, accounting, bored him to tears.

During one of Sam's late-night shifts at the restaurant, he met James Salvador, a local real-estate investor and developer well-known for his "$99 weekend real-estate seminars." Sam had waited on James in the restaurant several times during the previous couple of months. James had a magnetic personality that fascinated Sam. He always seemed to be the center of attention, and Sam couldn't help but notice the nice car he drove and the gold Rolex on his wrist. To Sam, James seemed to have it all together. James also took a liking to Sam and invited him to attend his next real-estate seminar nearby.

For Sam, $99 was a significant investment, but the hope of finding a shortcut to success while doing something he loved seemed more appealing than the accounting test coming up at 8:00 the next morning. Sam went home that night and Googled "how to make a million dollars selling real estate." He scanned the responses and found articles confirming that it was possible. Enthralled with the exciting stories of success, Sam was hooked. He knew he could do this, and he certainly knew it was going to be a lot more fun than studying accounting.

Fast-forward to six months later. Sam had dropped out of school, and his $99 weekend course turned into a $7,200 investment in additional "education" and "resources." He had tried to buy a couple of properties, but the bank denied his mortgage application both times. Maintaining his job at the restaurant while trying to get his real-estate investing career off the ground created stress and absolute exhaustion. James, his supposed mentor, turned out to be of little help and seemed to have no interest in Sam or his success. Sam realized that he bought into the most common scam around—the get-rich-quick scheme that turned out to be a get-poor-quick nightmare. He decided to give up his apartment, move back home with his parents, and reenter Lorain County Community College. *What a complete waste of time and money*, he thought while packing up his stuff.

THE CHALLENGES AND SOLUTIONS

Many great decisions are killed in the investigation process. Sam's decision to consider a career in real estate should not have started with a Google search for "how to make a million dollars in real estate" followed by a quick scan of results. The search term he chose biased the results in favor of the answer he was hoping to find—namely "it's easy!" If you want to find the *right* and *best* information for your investigations, you've got to learn how to search smarter.

Through my research and personal trial and error, I've discovered the six most common pitfalls that arise at the investigation stage in today's knowledge-rich world. Those errors are:

- **FAILURE TO BRAINSTORM:** If you followed the decision-making process outlined in chapter 1, you have made your decision—the one you are now investigating—based on a solid process that included unfiltered brainstorming. Similarly, the investigation phase needs to start with a different form of brainstorming that I'll discuss.

- **LOPSIDED QUESTIONING:** A key part of your investigation is simply asking the right questions. These questions can't be one-sided, totally success-oriented, or uninformed. You need to develop a solid list of diverse questions that approach the search from different angles and perspectives.

- **NARROW AND POOR-QUALITY SOURCES:** Utilizing only a small set of sources to guide your investigation and answer your questions is a dangerous pitfall. Using Google to find answers is an easy way to fall into this trap and can inadvertently cause you to rely on a poor-quality source. You must broaden your resources and sharpen your ability to recognize the junk sources that should be weeded out.

- **AVOIDING ACADEMIC RESOURCES:** The academic world may seem unapproachable or inaccessible, but there are quick and efficient ways to draw information from that sphere, where the accuracy of the information available is generally higher than that in most popular sources.

- **NO REAL-LIFE STORIES:** Sometimes the best way to conduct an investigation is to talk to people who have gone where you want to go. Speaking directly with other people and getting firsthand accounts of their experiences can be a vital part of your investigation.

- **ALL IN YOUR HEAD:** You need a sounding board. You will not realize how you are limiting yourself unless you speak with some people who will challenge your approach.

Now, let's examine each of these six pitfalls in more detail and learn specific strategies to avoid them by carrying out a balanced, productive investigation that provides a solid foundation for the next phase of the DISCIPLINE STRATEGY.

CHALLENGE: FAILURE TO BRAINSTORM

As we discussed in the previous chapter, brainstorming expands your thinking. In the decision step, we used brainstorming to expand the options being considered. Now, in the investigation phase, we use brainstorming to create a more robust list of questions. Failure to brainstorm at this point in the process is common and leads to limited thinking and incomplete investigation. As a result, we rely too heavily on the gleaming, glamorous-looking items that catch our attention in a limited search. These types of information are often the most skewed or inaccurate.

SOLUTION: DEVELOP A LIST OF CRITICAL QUESTIONS

The first step toward completing a thorough investigation is to brainstorm a list of questions. Just as in chapter 1, you should engage some friends or family in this effort. More brains typically mean more questions. You can use the same worksheet I provided at the end of chapter 1.

Going back to Sam's story as an example, we recall that he chose as his Google search phrase the extremely skewed "how to make a million dollars selling real estate." I just did that search myself. Of the ten results on page one, all but two were marketing books, seminars, or other get-rich-quick schemes. Two links were from reputable sources. One of those, from *Forbes* magazine, was surprisingly shallow. The other, from *The Wall Street Journal*, actually contained good information about the typical incomes of and challenges faced by real-estate professionals. However, Sam would have been likely to skip over any information that took a skeptical view of his predetermined goal of making a million dollars by selling real estate. That is why one must start with a broader list of questions that comes from brainstorming.

A brainstorming effort might include questions more specific to Sam's local environment, like "average Realtor income in Westlake, Ohio." This provides a link to the website salary.com, which shows the median income is $38,456 and that only 10 percent of realtors in his area earn over $58,439. These results may not necessarily deter Sam from his goal of making a million dollars in real estate, but they can help him set reasonable expectations for effort and time. Alternatively, Sam could have searched "how to be mentored as a Realtor." This search phrase just led me to an interesting set of links on how to approach the community's top agents and ask them to serve as a mentor. Those are two simple examples of questions that might result from a brainstorming session. Given the ease with which you can Google questions or statements, you should be able to create a long, unfiltered list of search terms and begin your investigation with your blinders off.

The easiest way to capture the information garnered is to copy each link found in your web search into a Word document or any note-taking application such as Evernote or OneNote and then type notes about each source under the link. Doing this will enable you to have easy access to your summary of the information and the actual source pages whenever you need it.

CHALLENGE: LOPSIDED QUESTIONING

Even after you develop a robust list of questions from your brainstorming session, the list may still be lopsided. This is due to a scientifically proven principle called "bias blindness."[1] Whether

---

1   Hansen, K., Gerbasi, M., Todorov, A., Kruse, E., & Pronin, E. (2014). People claim objectivity after knowingly using biased strategies. *Personality and Social Psychology Bulletin, 40*(6), 691-699.

you realize it or not, you have a bias regarding the decision you are researching. That bias is typically evident in how your brainstorming session evolves, but you will probably be blind to it. To fight this tendency, you must purposefully conduct searches with questions that go in the opposite direction of your beliefs or desires. This is not about being a negative person; rather, it means gathering information from many perspectives. We will discuss the issue of sifting through information in the next chapter. In the meantime, don't hesitate to gather information from a negative perspective. Just think how helpful it would have been for Sam to search "real estate million-dollar scam" or "James Salvador critical review."

SOLUTION: LOOK FOR OPPOSITES AND FIGHT IMPLICIT OR HIDDEN BIAS

Now that you have a long list of questions and statements from your brainstorming session, go back to that list and find the best *opposite* question or statement for each one. For example, an opposite approach to "how to lose twenty pounds" may be "common fad diets that don't work." This will give you a new perspective on the information you are gathering. It is a simple but effective technique for capturing additional points of view and sources.

A second way to avoid lopsided questioning is to anticipate and identify your implicit biases. *Explicit* biases are ones of which you are consciously aware, such as "I hate XYZ University and would never go there!" *Implicit*—or hidden—biases are ones that we are blind to on the surface but would probably be able to identify if we stopped to seriously think about it. They usually show up as *exclusions* from our thought process. When deciding upon a college, for example, it could be something as innocuous as failing to even consider community college as an option. The reasons for these biases may not be immediately apparent, so it takes some dedicated thinking to open our eyes to the options or information that's right under our noses.

The most difficult bias to counteract is implicit bias. This makes sense because, after all, these are usually the options we *don't see*. They can impact our judgment, behavior, and thinking without us ever realizing it. However, being aware of the issue and making a conscientious effort to find your implicit bias make you more likely to identify and overcome it.[2] Involving a friend or family member can improve your odds of identifying things that you haven't seen. Ask yourself these questions:

- What am I missing?
- How have I been biased in forming my questions?
- What have I excluded without even realizing it?
- What are the underlying assumptions in my list of questions?

After reviewing these questions carefully and possibly discussing them with friends, expand your list of questions to include new thoughts and ideas from your less-biased way of thinking.

CHALLENGE: NARROW AND POOR-QUALITY SOURCES

Earlier in this chapter, I recalled a story about my research years ago in high school. Back then, the challenge was to obtain enough sources to meet the modest expectations of a teacher or set of reviewers. Today you can gather information from numerous sources quickly, but there is no effective filtering mechanism, meaning you can wind up with a narrow group of sources that are often of poor quality.

The term *narrow sources* can mean two things. First, each source may present only a selective view based on its own biases. Second, you may find several sources, but they all only restate information from a third-party source, so the information is limited and redundant.

---

2 Milkman, K. L., Chugh, D., & Bazerman, M. H. (2009). How can decision making be improved?. Perspectives on psychological science, 4(4), 379-383.

Poor-quality content means that the information provided by the sources is based on flawed research, amounts only to opinion (though not identified as such), or purposefully misconstrues data to fulfill a predetermined purpose.

SOLUTION: VISIT YOUR LOCAL LIBRARY

Using the library is an obvious idea for most members of older generations, but many Internet-driven Millennials have never become familiar with their public library. So let's start at a very basic level.

In today's connected world, it may seem as if your local library and librarian have gone the way of the horse-drawn carriage. But, in fact, your local library system remains an excellent, free or very inexpensive way to help you find a broader set of resources.

The first step, of course, is to gain access to the resources there. This may require some type of registration or a library card. If possible, ask for a tour and an explanation of how the library can support your research effort. After this initial visit, you will know more about how your library operates and the extent of help available. You also can schedule time to meet with a librarian. Libraries are usually operated at the local level, even if they receive state support or oversight. The resources and experience available at a local library will vary tremendously across the country. Charles Sherrill, the State Librarian and Archivist for the State of Tennessee, recommends these tips on how to get up to speed on what your library has to offer:

- After visiting your library and getting oriented, use the electronic card catalog to conduct a search of available books and resources. Familiarize yourself with these materials. This initial work on your part shows that you are serious about what you are doing. The extent to which you present yourself as a serious researcher who has already done some initial work will greatly improve the assistance you receive.

Be prepared and as knowledgeable as possible before you first discuss your topic with the librarian.

- Introduce yourself to the librarian on duty, describe what you are researching, and ask who might be the best person to give you guidance. In a larger library, some librarians may have more experience with a topic than others.
- Realize the library and librarian may have broad access to materials and databases that you cannot search easily on your own. Librarians enjoy the research process and will be eager to assist.
- The librarian may continue to do research after your initial meeting and follow up with additional thoughts. Be responsive to any follow-up.
- If your first experience with a librarian is not positive for whatever reason, don't give up. Look for an opportunity to work with another librarian at that location or visit another branch of the library.[3]

I realize all this may sound elementary to some readers, but I've worked with enough college students and twenty-somethings to know library research is quickly becoming a lost art in our modern world.

CHALLENGE: AVOIDING ACADEMIC SOURCES

Most people do not perceive the academic world of university-level research as accessible. However, it is actually more accessible now than in the past, thanks mainly to Google Scholar. Although it would take significant training to understand some of the scientific and statistical methods utilized in these research studies, you don't have to be an expert to comprehend the conclusions reached. Research papers present an abstract summarizing

---

3   From a verbal interview with Charles A. Sherrill, State Librarian and Archivist for the State of Tennessee.

their findings and conclusions, permitting the non-professional researcher to gain guidance and insight from the work.

SOLUTION: PAY ATTENTION TO THE ABSTRACT

Let me give you a simple example that demonstrates how to use Google Scholar and the information it provides about research studies. As I write this, I am fifty-four years old and enjoy weight training with a professional trainer. My trainer suggests that I drink a whey protein shake with added creatine and omega-3 fatty acids. This is a specific mix of ingredients that he has figured out over his forty years of competitive weightlifting and training thousands of individuals. I want to determine for myself whether there is any academic evidence that these ingredients will have an impact on my resistance training efforts.

So let's investigate each topic—whey protein, creatine, and omega-3 fatty acids—and see how they relate to muscle development as a result of resistance training. My whey-protein search is shown as an example below.

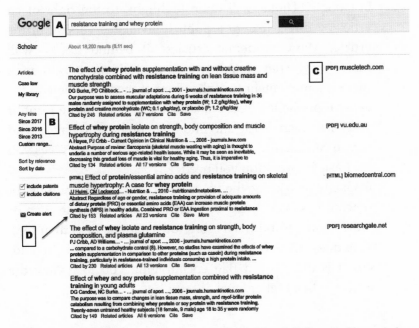

- **STEP I:** Go to https://scholar.google.com/
- **STEP 2:** Determine, to the best of your ability, a good search term. You can try several possibilities until you get a good list of research studies that appear relevant to your search. For the topic of whey protein, I used the search term "resistance training and whey protein."
- **STEP 3:** Review the results of the search.

My search results are shown here. Let's take a look at the four key elements I've indicated on the screen shot.

- **A:** Your search term or phrase will have a significant impact on the results produced. As mentioned in STEP 2, vary your search term until it produces a robust list of relevant studies.
- **B:** On the left side is a list of options that let you control the time period for your search. I recommend defining a window of time that covers the past five years. Recent research is built on previous research, either verifying or challenging previous studies. The last five-year period typically gives you the most accurate overview of a topic.
- **C:** Google Scholar will often highlight, to the right of an article, a direct link to a publicly available version of the article. Many academic articles sit behind a pay wall (meaning you have to pay to view the full reports), although there is a movement to make more of them available to the general public for free. Look for these links to the right. If you click on an article and find that you have to pay to read it, you can usually access an abstract for free that gives you the basic information you need.
- **D:** One way to judge the value of an article is the number of times it has been cited. Be wary of articles that are two or more years old but have very few citations (less than ten). This does not necessarily mean the information is invalid, but it is often a red flag encouraging you to review the article with a higher level of scrutiny.

Click on at least ten highly cited articles found on the first couple pages of search results. Read the abstract for each and, if available, the conclusion. This will not be a lot of reading, but it will give you a firm grasp of credible research.

To continue with the whey protein example, let's look at the article from the *International Journal of Sport Nutrition and Exercise Metabolism*. When I click on this link, I am presented with the name of the journal that published the article and an abstract of the article. A PDF copy of the article is available for purchase. Generally, you will need to purchase an article only if you determine that it contains critical information to support your investigation. Before you make a purchase, you should return to the search results, click on the link "all 13 versions" (the number will vary with the article), and see if a free version is available elsewhere.

The abstract for our selected article is shown here, with the information most critical for my purposes highlighted in bold underline:

Different dietary proteins affect whole body protein anabolism and accretion and therefore, have the potential to influence results obtained from resistance training. This study examined the effects of supplementation with two proteins, **hydrolyzed whey isolate (WI)** and casein (C), on strength, body composition, and plasma glutamine levels during a 10 wk, supervised resistance training program. In a double-blind protocol, 13 male, recreational bodybuilders supplemented their normal diet with either WI or C (1.5 gm/kg body wt/d) for the duration of the program. Strength was assessed by 1-RM in three exercises (barbell bench press, squat, and cable pull-down). Body composition was assessed by dual energy X-ray absorptiometry. Plasma glutamine levels were determined by the enzymatic method with spectrophotometric detection. All assessments occurred in the week before and the week following 10 wk of training. Plasma glutamine levels did not change in either supplement group following the intervention. **The WI group achieved a significantly greater gain ($p \le$**

0.01) in lean mass than the C group (5.0 ± 0.3 vs. 0.8 ± 0.4 kg for WI and C, respectively) and a significant ($p < 0.05$) change in fat mass (-1.5 ± 0.5 kg) compared to the C group ($+0.2 \pm 0.3$ kg). **The WI group also achieved significantly greater ($p \leq$ 0.05) improvements in strength** compared to the C group in each assessment of strength. When the strength changes were expressed relative to body weight, the WI group still achieved significantly greater ($p < 0.05$) improvements in strength compared to the C group.[4]

Remember, this article is just one piece of the puzzle. But the abstract alone tells me that whey isolate (i.e., whey protein) has a positive impact on lean mass and strength. The scientific language or the math should not intimidate you. Simply look for the conclusions, which will be stated in relatively plain English.

Finally, you can check the legitimacy of the source by looking up the H-Index of the journal that published the article. This index is a simple measure of a journal's influence. There are some sketchy journals in the world that will publish anything; you want to rely on respectable journals, and the H-Index is an easy way for you to determine respectability. You can find the H-Index for all journals by visiting the Scimago Journal & Country Rank page (www.scimagojr.com/journalrank.php). Simply enter your journal's title and you will be presented with some summary information about it, with the H-Index being most prominent. As noted previously, the journal in this instance is the *International Journal of Sport Nutrition and Exercise Metabolism*. The H-Index for the journal is 52. I will spare you the technical details, but the number means that there are 52 articles with at least 52 citations. There is no set cutoff as to what is acceptable, but the H-Index is a good way to compare the relative strength of the different journals. Of course,

---

4   P.J. Cribb, A.D. Williams, M.F. Carey, and A. Hayes, "The effect of whey isolate and resistance training on strength, body composition, and plasma glutamine," International Journal of Sport Nutrition and Exercise Metabolism, October, 2006, https://www.ncbi.nlm.nih.gov/pubmed/17240782#.

higher scores are better. I tend to scrutinize with greater care any article from a journal with an H-Index of 10 or less.

It is unwise to avoid academic research. With the brief introduction above, you should now feel comfortable including Google Scholar in your investigation. This will bring a whole new depth and dimension to whatever topic you'll explore from this point on.

CHALLENGE: NO REAL-LIFE STORIES

No true research should be complete without including the real-life stories of people who have firsthand experience with the topic you're researching. Most of us are reluctant to reach out to someone we don't know, but most people with experience and interest in whatever you're researching will be eager to share their stories with you. Nothing you find online or in a book can replace this type of feedback. Always keep in mind, though, that these people can only speak from their personal experiences. This means their stories may not be precisely relevant to your situation.

SOLUTION: LEARN HOW TO NETWORK

Because of my professional role as an entrepreneur and business owner, I am contacted by someone seeking career advice at least once a month. I'm always happy to receive messages from younger professionals who are trying to build their network. It shows they're serious about expanding their knowledge base and finding new avenues for research and investigation. There are many great ways to improve your networking ability but let me cover the three best ways I know of right now: LinkedIn, niche forums, and personal networking.

LINKEDIN

Most people find me through LinkedIn, a social network for professionals. If you are not familiar with it, visit www.LinkedIn. com. You can easily set up your account and profile for free. It's a great way to expand your network by reaching the people your current friends, colleagues, and business acquaintances know.

My response to people who contact me through LinkedIn is always positive, as I believe is typical. These are usually hungry young professionals making an honest effort to expand their opportunities and make a mark on the world. If they're interested in an area I'm familiar with or involved in, I'll usually invite them to my office and set up meetings with a variety of associates in my consulting firm.

To reach out to people on LinkedIn, you must first set up an account and post your online résumé. This is free but should be undertaken with some care and effort to present your educational background and your interests favorably. This environment works well for people looking for career information. You may also find other types of advice on business startups and midlife career changes through LinkedIn. Contact people of interest by messaging them through LinkedIn or by obtaining their contact information after you have "connected" with them. If you are going to send a connection request to people, be sure to explain why you are connecting to them when you make the request. I get a lot of requests on LinkedIn that don't make sense to me, and I don't accept those connections. However, if someone takes the time to explain that he or she is connecting to obtain career ideas or other advice, I will accept their connection request.

In many cases, once you have connected with someone through LinkedIn, you should follow up with a request for a phone conversation or meeting. In effect, you are asking this person to provide mentoring. The information obtained in these interactions can be priceless. You have the opportunity to hear insights and wisdom that a more experienced person has developed over decades, including their failures and successes. In the bonus resources listed at the end of this chapter, you'll find a Mentor Discussion Guide worksheet to help you prepare for a meeting with your mentor. Of course, LinkedIn is not the only mechanism through which you can find mentors. You should also consider personal relationships, professional organizations, and other networks that may be unique to you.

NICHE FORUMS

Niche forums offer another, although slightly less personal, way to meet people virtually and receive excellent advice. I participate in two such forums. As a pilot and airplane owner, I participate in a forum for people who own a similar type of airplane. These forums provide an opportunity to pose questions to a group of people with relevant experience who can help me find answers to difficult questions. Some of this information is opinion-based but in a high-quality forum all opinions are expressed respectfully and debated openly, enabling you to reach your own conclusions. The information found in such a forum is typically not available anywhere else.

I also participate in a heart health forum. Since I have a family history of heart disease, I am passionate about maintaining the best cardiovascular and overall health possible. I have a good doctor, but that is only one piece of the puzzle; I also like to benefit from multiple sources of expert guidance. The heart health forum provides access to several hundred individuals' experiences, research, and recommendations.

Although I prefer niche forums, you also can find some decent information through subcategories of larger forums. For example, the websites Reddit and Quora typically provide information and personal experience on practically any topic you can think of. However, this can be challenging territory to navigate since there is no barrier to entry and no monitoring. As a result, a lot of useless or commercially motivated information can enter these forums. In my experience niche forums that require some type of membership fee provide the highest quality of information.

PERSONAL NETWORKING

The extent to which personal networking will help you depends on the strength of your network of friends, acquaintances, colleagues, and family members. However, most people under-estimate the power of their personal network. Once you start asking the people in your network if they know anyone who does *this* or has experience with *that*, you may be surprised how easy it is to get connected to a person with the right experience and knowledge to help you. The point is to ask everyone you know for help.

When you arrange a personal conversation with people whom you reach through any of these means, you should have a clear purpose and be well-prepared for the conversation to gain the greatest possible benefit. The worksheet provided at the end of this chapter is designed to guide you through that conversation.

CHALLENGE: ALL IN YOUR HEAD

You have now conducted a complete investigation to gather data and advice. Perhaps you encountered a serious hurdle or concern that will cause you to return to the first step and reconsider your decision. This may not happen often (at least, it hasn't in my experience), but you have to be open to the possibility and deal with it maturely—which means accepting reality, starting over, and making a new decision. Such a situa-tion occurred when I was in college. I grew up wanting to be a fighter pilot. I studied and trained to earn a military scholarship to college, but one day, I learned I had imperfect color vision. I knew from my research into military flying that this was a hurdle I could not overcome. It marked the end of my military flying hopes and required a new life decision. Before I went off in a new direction, however, I knew I needed to talk through the problem with trusted friends and mentors. The ordeal had been a nightmare for me, and I needed to get the level-headed insights of people I respected.

You see, the investigation process is sometimes a solo journey. And, depending on the nature of the decision you are investigating, it can be a highly emotional and complex journey. This may lead you to become rather withdrawn and hyper-focused on the task at hand of learning everything you can possibly learn! But, as a result, you lose the benefit of an independent third party who might help you avoid unhealthy ways of thinking, or obvious missteps in your thinking. If none of your thought processes are ever spoken out loud and discussed with others, you will unknowingly limit the quality of your investigation.

Therefore, the final step in the investigation process, which can occur at any time during the process, is to get out of your head and talk through what you have learned with friends and family.

SOLUTION: TALK IT OUT WITH FRIENDS AND FAMILY WHO WILL CHALLENGE YOU

As we observed in the previous chapter, the mind is not always our best friend. Our web of deceit can skew our perception. You have to get out of your head, talk with others, and let people challenge your thinking. Being open to challenge is a required skill for any professional. Do not put up a defensive wall against challenges; if your decision and the information you have gathered from your investigation don't stand up to scrutiny, then you have a problem. Be open, discuss, and listen to others' feedback. These conversations may cause you to reinitiate your investigative effort in search of more information because someone questioned or challenged your thinking. Now you are on a quest to understand the challenge more fully and either counteract it with facts or factor it into your better-informed view of the topic.

INVESTIGATING FOR SUCCESS

The investigation process can be both fun and tiring, thrilling and exhausting. The goal is to get your hands on and head around any piece of data that can help inform your decision and lead you to a solid plan for putting your decision into action. Simply gathering all the information, however, is not enough. Before you can conceive your plan, you must first sort through all the great (and possibly not-so-great) information you collected during your investigation. That's a critical part of the process, and one you cannot afford to skip. We'll cover that crucial sorting process next.

———— TAKE IT FURTHER ————

Be sure to download these worksheets from www.
DISCIPLINESTRATEGY.com to put what you've learned in this
chapter into action immediately!

Unfiltered Brainstorming

This worksheet, also used in chapter 1, guides you through the
process of a brainstorming session and provides guidelines and
prompts to stimulate discussion.

Mentor Discussion Guide

This worksheet is designed to guide you through your meeting or
discussion with someone who is assisting you in your search for
information.

CHAPTER 3

SORT

*"I will look at any additional evidence to confirm
the opinion to which I have already come."*
—Lord Molson

A fter the first two steps of the DISCIPLINE STRATEGY process,
you may be feeling information overload. You have gathered a
lot of good information and have had many discussions with
people about your decision. Now you are looking at a mound
of information and wondering how to turn it into a meaningful
knowledge base. This third step in *DISCIPLINE STRATEGY* may
not be the most glamorous one, but it is a critical step in the process.

Twentieth-century British politician Lord Molson once said,
"I will look at any additional evidence to confirm the opinion
to which I have already come." This is exactly how we will *not*
do things in this phase of the process. Sorting information is not
about finding material that confirms our biases; it is about moving
forward with an open mind and expanding our understanding of
the challenges that lie ahead.

As discussed in the previous chapter, we all have biases that impact how we view the information we have gathered. In this sorting step of the DISCIPLINE STRATEGY, you will learn how to determine which sources are trustworthy, how to best weave the information together, and how the information will form the basis for the plan you will conceive in the next step. This is a nuts-and-bolts chapter that focuses on a straightforward process for organizing your information.

THE GROUND-LEVEL VIEW
(WHAT THIS LOOKS LIKE IN REAL LIFE)

Alicia felt like she had been "soaring on the wings of change" for the past couple weeks. Even her self-talk had become inspired. She was certain she was on the path to finally making a career change she had dreamed about for over a year. She had collected more than one hundred web links, downloaded sixty-five PDF documents, and had email exchanges with five different professionals in her new career. Her investigation phase had been a success!

But now, she feels overwhelmed. Looking back over her web links, she doesn't remember why she thought they were so good at the time. She made a few cryptic notes, but she no longer recalls what they meant. When she downloaded the PDF documents, she didn't realize that file names like "930-zyekw.pdf" were useless. Now she has a large number of files and no idea what each one contains. In the initial joy of finding all this great material, she thought every piece was valuable; now she thinks, *This is all just a waste of my time. What am I doing? How in the world do I make sense of this mess?*

THE CHALLENGES AND SOLUTIONS

In the investigation phase of the DISCIPLINE STRATEGY, I outlined a process designed to help you gather balanced information from a variety of viewpoints. Now that you have a significant amount of information, your challenge is figuring out how to turn it into an organized and useful summary that will guide planning and implementation. You will face several problems in this process. When you actually conceive your plan in the next chapter, you will be exercising very high-level thinking skills. But that successful thinking will be built on the critical foundation of a solid, broad, organized knowledge base you have developed. Or, to put it simply, your decisions tomorrow will only be as good as the information you gather and process today. So don't skip this step!

As we've done for the first two steps, let's start by taking a high-level view of the four biggest challenges in the sorting phase:

- **YOUR BELIEF SYSTEM:** Your brain, specifically the amygdala, reacts to an intellectual challenge just as it does to a physical threat. Your core beliefs, which may be challenged in this data-sorting phase, tend to be very rigid. This may prevent you from viewing the data objectively.

- **RETICULAR ACTIVATING SYSTEM:** Your reticular activating system (RAS) operates like a traffic cop, managing the massive amount of information and stimuli that bombard you throughout the day. Your conscious mind can be used to activate this powerful filter and communicate with your subconscious mind. This can work *for* you or *against* you. I'll help you make sure that you utilize your RAS to your advantage.

- **CREDIBILITY:** In discussing the investigation phase, I mentioned the issues of quality and credibility, but I did not emphasize these heavily so as not to slow down or narrow your search process. However, now you must make some decisions concerning the credibility of your sources.

- **ORGANIZING:** Unless you have a lot of experience in organizing information, this activity might seem overwhelming. You can't let this become a stumbling block, though, so we will look at technical tools you can use and a specific step-by-step organizing process.

Those are the key pitfalls we need to avoid, so let's break them down and get a better look at the challenges and solutions for each one.

CHALLENGE: YOUR BELIEF SYSTEM

A recent study by the Brain and Creativity Institute at the University of Southern California showed that a person who holds firmly to a belief typically has no flexibility or openness to contrary evidence that might call that belief into question. Political and religious convictions are at the top of the list of beliefs we usually find difficult to change. So while your favorite vegetable may be open for discussion, your political or religious beliefs are likely fixed and inflexible. In our process, the decision you are researching falls somewhere between those two extremes. Whether you realize it or not, you probably already have a set of beliefs related to the topic at hand, so how do you stay open to new information and remain flexible in your thought process?

SOLUTION: NURTURE OPEN-MINDEDNESS

Jason Baehr, a philosophy professor at Loyola Marymount University, found:

> An open-minded person is characteristically (a) willing and (within limits) able (b) to transcend a default cognitive standpoint (c) in order to take up or take seriously the merits of (d) a distinct cognitive standpoint.[5]

More simply, open-minded people are genuinely able to consider new information and use it to revise the beliefs they held prior to receiving the new information. As such, open-minded people tend to be smart. However, it is not clear which comes first:

---

5 Jason Baehr, "The Structure of Open-Mindedness," Loyola Marymount University, January 1, 2011, https://digitalcommons.lmu.edu/cgi/viewcontent.cgi?referer=https://www.google.com/&httpsredir=1&article=1024&context=phil_fac.

the open-mindedness or the intelligence. Either way, you should recognize the value of being open-minded and nurture that attribute during the sorting process. But how?

First, it is easier to be open-minded when you are not stressed or under time pressure. Sorting information should happen when you feel energetic and fresh. Open-mindedness takes willpower, which is a finite resource. Give yourself both time and a relaxed environment in which to consider the information you are sorting.

Second, listen to the perspectives of others. Your information-gathering phase included networking and talking to potential mentors or people who had experience and knowledge related to your decision. Reconsider those conversations and how you might have filtered out views contrary to yours. Stop and consider those more openly now.

Third, the importance you place on your decision will influence your open-mindedness. People tend to be more open-minded when they realize the significance of the topic. Think about the positive impact your decision will have on your life and about the importance of considering all viewpoints.

Open-mindedness is a conscious decision. Most people are not aware of the degree to which we protect previously formed beliefs. In your workspace, place a large note or sign reading, "STAY OPEN-MINDED." This will help you keep both your conscious and subconscious mind more attuned to new and perhaps belief-challenging information.

CHALLENGE: RETICULAR ACTIVATING SYSTEM

As I said, your reticular activating system manages the seemingly endless information and stimuli that bombards your brain every day. It tells you what is worth focusing on and what you should ignore. Robert M. Sapolsky, in his book *Behave: The Biology of Humans at Our Best and Worst*, provides a detailed and fascinating eight hundred-page account of how our brains work. The complexity he describes gives insight into just how difficult it is to keep our subconscious mind from quietly determining where our conscious mind focuses. One way to leverage the power of the subconscious mind is by planting specific goals or thoughts into our subconscious through visualization and goal-setting. The challenge here is that you have *already* programmed your subconscious—whether you realize it or not. You need new programming that will support your new decision.

SOLUTION: USE SPECIFIC GOALS, INTENTIONALITY, AND VISUALIZATION

Your RAS is always on, functioning as your vigilant filter of all sensory information, even when we don't realize it. If you start thinking about buying a new Ford Mustang, you will suddenly begin to notice every Ford Mustang on the road. If you have a specific problem on your mind and are flipping through a magazine or web page, you may notice what seems to be the perfect answer to that problem. Think of your subconscious mind, and specifically your RAS, as a powerful computer that you can program and use to your advantage.

If you start sorting through your information, old programming in your RAS will immediately begin filtering your material and bringing certain items to the forefront of your awareness. But, since you have made a decision that most likely is taking you in a new direction, you need to reprogram your RAS to serve you best. Here is how to do that.

Start by writing your specific goals and some detailed sub-goals on some large notecards or pieces of paper. The more detail you can provide, the better. These written goals will be visible throughout your sorting process. Under each detailed goal, explain why you are going to achieve this goal. You are setting your intent and positively programming your RAS by doing this. The language you use is important, so write these in a positive and intentional way. For example, say you want to run a marathon. Which of the following three written goals would work best?

I hope to finish a marathon someday.
I want to complete a marathon next year.
I intend to complete the Walt Disney World Marathon on January 10, 2021.

The third version is much more specific than the others and gives your brain more detailed information to work with. With this goal, your RAS can begin focusing on crossing a specific finish line on a specific day instead of "some day."

Underneath each of these goals, you may have sub-goals with even more detail. The intentionality comes from the specifics, phrased in a positive way, that you add into the detail of each sub-goal. In our marathon example, you might craft a sub-goal that says:

I will commit to the training schedule I adopt and will celebrate the completion of each training run by walking through my backyard garden with a glass of chocolate milk while reflecting on my positive progress toward my goal.

Whether or not you have a backyard garden, you get the point: put a lot of detail into your goal. In this example, your sorting process would involve deciding what training program works best for you, along with many other decisions about how to reach your goal.

Finally, use visualization to further cement the programming of your RAS. I like vision boards. My wife and I have both used these extensively to program our RAS and maintain laser-focus on what we are looking for and what will support our goals despite the constant flood of sensory overload.

Following are some fun examples of vision boards to give you a sense of how elaborate or simple they can be.

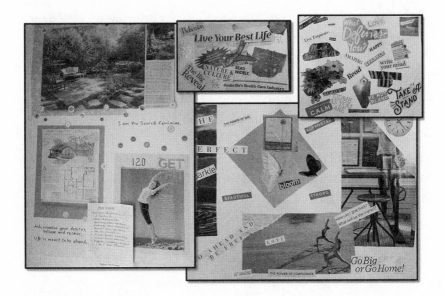

CHALLENGE: CREDIBILITY

We touched briefly on the issue of judging quality and credibility during the investigation chapter, but we were at that point referring mostly to academic material. When you get to sorting, you now have a variety of information in front of you and must decide what is reliable.

In the following sorting and organizing process, you will give each piece of research a tag indicating its level of credibility. This is certainly not an easy task in today's world of "fake news," so we will discuss it in detail before moving on to the nuts and bolts of sorting and organizing.

SOLUTION: TAKE TIME TO CONSIDER THE SOURCE

You must be rather cold-hearted when eliminating poor-quality information. You may have found some information that sounds appealing and hope it has some validity. To continue with our marathon example, one source might tell you that you only need to run one day a week to train for your first marathon. That may sound good, but the source is a website for a supplement company that is simply trying to sell its product, not offering real guidance on marathon training.

Before getting into the sorting process, you should review all your sources of information and make notes that will help you give each one a credibility rating as outlined in the next section. The following are some features to look for.

HIGHLY CREDIBLE SITES

Websites that are government-affiliated, referenced by the Library of Congress, or connected with peer-reviewed journals can be considered highly credible.

1. Is the information from an official government website? You can find a list of such sources for US sites at https://www.usa.gov/federal-agencies/.
2. Is the source from one of the reference sites selected by the Library of Congress? These are found at http://www.loc.gov/rr/askalib/virtualref.html.
3. Is the source from a respected academic journal? A very robust list is maintained at http://www.scimagojr.com/journalrank.php.

In addition to these sites, any website ending in .gov, .edu, .us, or .mil is highly likely to be legitimate. These domain extensions are restricted (with the exception of .us) to official government, educational, or military institutions. While technically anyone can obtain the .us extension, it is most commonly used by local state and city governments.

NEWS AND MAGAZINE ARTICLES

News and magazines are difficult to judge due to the prevalence of opinion pieces and articles designed simply to generate web traffic and ad revenue. Those news or magazine articles that contain good information usually refer to another source, a personal interview, an academic journal, or some published research finding. If possible, dig deeper and find the original source. It is not as common as it once was to find news or magazine articles that contain original material. Find the source and consider its entire content.

BLOGS AND OPINION SITES

Blogs and opinion sites can be a good source of information when the authors are experts in the field they are discussing. Research the person writing the blog or opinion by checking the "About" page of their site, doing a Google search for their name, reading biographical information, and considering reviews. I have found that some of the most cutting-edge and useful information can be found on these types of sites, but their credibility is often uneven. So look carefully at the website. How does it appear? Is it selling products of questionable value or promoting a particular viewpoint, sharing valuable information for the good of humanity, or something in between? Your intuition and judgment will be necessary to make a determination. Stay open-minded and take the time needed to evaluate the source carefully. And never discount a site merely because it presents a point of view that cuts against your biases. Remember, your goal is to take in *all* the relevant information—even that which challenges your preexisting beliefs.

SCHOLARLY MATERIAL

I discussed how to locate and evaluate scholarly material in the previous chapter. Most of the information contained in academic journals will be solid. However, occasionally a research study may be supported by an organization with a particular agenda. As I mentioned previously, use the ratings for the journal and the number of citations of the articles as a quick way to judge the credibility of this material.

MEMBER-ONLY SITES

There are thousands of topic-focused, member-only sites where high-quality forum discussions sit behind a pay wall. These can be outstanding sources of information. Membership fees are fairly reasonable, especially if you are joining for only a short period of time to access information during a search.

Most of the information on these sites comes from firsthand experience, which can make it difficult to gauge its credibility if you don't know the people. However, you can still use their experiences—not to mention the number of people who support a particular view or teaching—to measure the impact of the site's content. You'll no doubt also find plenty of conflicting opinions in these forum discussions that further complicate your credibility assessment, but this isn't necessarily a problem. The goal for these sites should be to use the discussions as a sounding board to help gauge the information you find on other, more credible sources.

CHALLENGE: ORGANIZING—AN IMPOSING TASK

The way we organize information is usually driven by our personal preferences. Some people believe they already have strong organizational skills while others are content to live in a little disarray. You need to come up with a system that works for you. Therefore, I will outline a process, but I encourage you to personalize it. Whatever you do, though, don't shortchange this activity.

SOLUTION: A STEP-BY-STEP PROCESS FOR SORTING AND ORGANIZING INFORMATION

At this point, your momentum may be waning if the conflicting information seems overwhelming. When you made your decision, your brain gave you a big shot of motivating dopamine. This neurotransmitter is as potent and uplifting as any manmade drug. It has probably energized your search and given you the mental fuel to get to this point, but now it may be starting to subside. This is normal! Doubts and a sense of exhaustion at this phase are typical, but you can maintain (or regain) your momentum by following a clear, effective process for organizing all the great information you've gathered. The following is my suggested process that you can customize and personalize for yourself.

STEP 1: Change Your Environment

Get out of your kitchen, office, library, study, or wherever you have been planted for the past several days of researching. A different setting will help you focus and break out of old thought patterns. At the very least, pack up your stuff and move to the local coffee shop. Order your favorite beverage, put your headphones on if you wish, and start assessing your accumulated research. If possible, take a weekend trip to your favorite getaway location like the mountains or the beach.

STEP 2: Expect Conflicting Information

As I mentioned earlier, Google prioritizes information based on trustworthiness and popularity. Some sites pay Google to earn a spot on the top search results, and Google tags those sites with "Ad." Unfortunately, some less-scrupulous organizations have learned how to game this system. As a result, a search like the one on the following page on "how to retire early" may result in contradictions, lots of ads, and cheesy "clickbait" articles on the first page.

You may have thought some of the less-credible data still had potential usefulness and therefore captured that data during your investigation. That's okay. No matter how you found the information, there will be some conflicts among sources. Remember, we are working on being open-minded during this sorting process.

STEP 3: Decide on a Method That Works for You

Some people can manage volumes of information electronically. If that works for you, great! You might consider using these tools:

- **Microsoft Office or Google Docs:** You can do a lot with Microsoft Word, Excel, and even Access if you are a Microsoft-savvy individual. Google Docs offers a similar set of free tools online. I won't direct you to any specific resources on how to use these tools because the Internet is full of good YouTube videos and documents explaining how to use them to organize information.

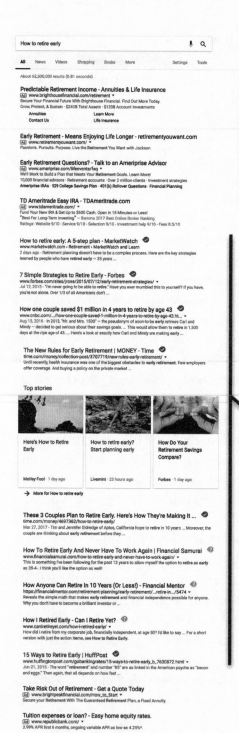

Advertisements. They are attempting to sell you a product, thus the advice is biased.

Short, pop culture articles designed to sell magazines and get you to click on their page. Much of it conflicts and none of it is very helpful when designing a plan to retire early.

Google and the Google logo are registered trademarks of Google LLC, used with permission.

- **Evernote:** This very intuitive tool allows the sorting and grouping of many types of information. A basic version is free; an expanded version costs a small fee per year. Visit www.evernote.com.

- **OneNote:** This is a robust note-taking and archiving tool from Microsoft with great options for desktop computing, phone, and tablet apps. OneNote is especially good at saving websites with a browser extension and then marking them up in a new note inside the application. It can also be enhanced by a number of third-party apps and integrates well with other Microsoft Office products. Microsoft offers this tool free to all users whether they have a paid Microsoft Office account or not. Visit www.onenote.com.

- **Trello:** Trello is often used in software development and works well in that arena. I have used it in my software businesses, and it functions effectively as a team tool. It is very easy to use, and I especially like the ease of rearranging information as you are sorting. The individual version is free. Visit www.trello.com.

- **BaseCamp:** I used BaseCamp effectively several years ago, soon after it was first released. However, it has recently changed its business model to focus less on individual users and more on corporate clients. As such, at least at the time of this writing, individual use is limited to teachers and students. If you fall into one of those categories, BaseCamp is a very powerful and robust tool. If you are not a teacher or student, access may be difficult without a corporate license, which is cost-prohibitive for most people. To investigate further, visit www.basecamp.com.

- **Paper:** There is also the ancient tool, invented in 105 A.D. in China, called *paper*. Yes, some people still use pencil and paper for their research and sorting! Something about it can't be replaced by electronic tools. I still find writing things on paper or using large pads to sort and organize information to be incredibly effective. Don't be embarrassed about sticking with this traditional method if it suits your needs. Also, small sticky notes are great for tagging material, as we will discuss shortly.

STEP 4: The Sorting Process

Gathering information can often seem like a flurry of discovery, with each additional piece of information striking you as more interesting than the last. Now, in order to sort your research, you have to read *everything*! As you read, you will decide how to classify each item based on several categories. Whether you are using an electronic or a paper-based system, you'll need to tag each piece of information. A tag is a naming convention that you invent and apply to information. Each piece of information can have multiple tags. I will give several tag examples below. Feel free to revise this list as you deem necessary.

- **Tag Topic: Credibility**
  Tag Labels: low, medium, high
  Credibility can be judged in several ways. First, who is providing the information? What can you find out about the author from a Google search or other sources? Does he or she qualify as an expert? Is the material geared to sell you something? If so, its credibility may be in doubt. Copy a sentence from the material and paste it into Google to search for other uses of the sentence. Is this material original, or has it been copied from another source?

- **Tag Topic: Detail Level**
  Tag Labels: none, low, medium, high
  Shallow articles are popular among many print and web-based magazines. Personally, I find these sources rarely provide enough detail to be of much use. I would therefore label them as having no or low detail. Highly detailed information can be surprisingly difficult to find despite the overwhelming amount of data on the Internet. When you find a source of this kind, tag it as such so you don't lose track of

it. If you are researching early retirement, for example, you will find hundreds of articles in personal-finance magazines that contain fewer than five hundred words and nothing of substance. However, J. P. Morgan has a PDF on its web site concerning early retirement that is fifty pages long and tremendously detailed.

- **Tag Topic: Subjective Measure of Reasonableness**
  Tag Labels: not reasonable, questionable, reasonable
  This subjective estimate of reasonableness may seem contrary to the goal of maintaining open-mindedness, but it is not. Being open-minded means you are not rejecting information without careful consideration in light of full awareness of your own biases. But some information just isn't reasonable, or it may be perfectly reasonable for *some* people but not for your personal situation. Therefore, reasonableness may be a global or personal evaluation. Sticking with the example of early retirement, one article on the topic suggests moving to Ecuador. If you have strong roots in your community or family, this option may get a "not reasonable" tag regardless of the financial or other benefits of relocating to South America.

- **Tag Topic: Opinion, Science, Fact**
  Tag Labels: authoritative opinion, opinion, science, fact
  It is important to distinguish fact from opinion. An authoritative opinion comes from someone whom you consider an authority on the topic, one for whose opinions you have high regard. For example, I follow the work of a couple of medical doctors who have written books and maintain blogs. I consider them authoritative and give their opinions careful consideration. However, other people about whose opinions I know nothing are labeled as simply "opinion" in my sorting process.

Science and fact may seem similar, but there is a key difference. Science is any research study or statement of scientific observation that is not expressed as an opinion. Since science is always being challenged and is evolving, it differs from fact. Facts, such as the population of Ecuador or the distance from the earth to the moon, are indisputable.

- **Tag Topic: Emotional Enthusiasm**
  Tag Labels: boring, resonates, exciting
  Emotional enthusiasm is an important ingredient that should not be ignored. If a research article strikes you as totally uninspiring, you should mark it as boring. This does not mean the information will not be helpful, but you may find other information with similar content that is more suited to your tastes. When an information source resonates, you have an intuitive conviction that it makes sense and somehow fits into the puzzle of information you are accumulating. You may not totally understand why a particular source resonates with you, but you should identify and note it. Finally, any information that strikes you as exciting may give you some insight into what will keep you motivated for the long haul.

- **Tag Topic: Theme/Topic**
  Tag Labels: (varies by topic) early retirement topic might include tags for downsizing, living on less, how to save more, best communities
  The theme is specific to your particular context or subject matter and may become evident only as you read the material. Take side notes on possible themes and, as you see a trend emerging, you can go back and label the items accordingly. If a young entrepreneur is deciding whether to start a restaurant franchise, several themes might emerge such as startup capital, marketing assistance, training, and so on.

- **Tag Topic: Date**
  Tag Labels: more than 5 years old, 1–5 years old, less than 1 year old
  Your topic influences the relevance of how recent an article is. You may want to assess the relevance of the date of each publication and perhaps create date groupings. The sample tags should be arranged in time segments that make sense for your topic. For example, if you are a Type 2 diabetic and decide that you want to attempt to reverse this condition through lifestyle changes, then material published thirty years ago will be much less helpful than more recent research. Finding the tipping point in terms of recency on a given topic is not always obvious. For medical or technology-related research, I would suggest putting more emphasis on the past five years because change happens so fast in these fields. Other topics may have relevant information stretching back decades.

STUDY, TAKE NOTES, AND FORM A FOUNDATION

This chapter on sorting information and the previous chapter on investigating are all about discovering new material and integrating it into your brain. You now have to take time to become proficient with the topic and your research. Read everything again. Note particularly the material that scored well during the sorting process. This information is high in credibility and detail, authoritative or scientifically based, exciting, and timely. Make notes as a general summary of the information that will serve as your foundation.

This is the end of Phase 1 of the DISCIPLINE STRATEGY. You have made a decision; you have conducted a thorough investigation; you have sorted through a large amount of material; and finally you have summarized and reviewed that material until it is part of you. You should feel knowledgeable about your decision at this point, confident that you have formed a solid, research-based belief system concerning your decision and how to move forward. The next step is where things *really* get moving: it's time to conceive your plan. This is a magical part of the process, and we'll cover that next.

———— TAKE IT FURTHER ————

You have a lot of work to do during the sorting step, but I've created a thorough worksheet to help you make the most of your time. Visit www.DISCIPLINESTRATEGY.com now to download the worksheet for this chapter.

Sort Worksheet

The Sort Worksheet serves as a reference when sorting material. It helps you walk each piece of data through your belief system, reticular activating system, credibility analysis, and the organizational process. It also summarizes the tagging scheme and will help you grade your materials consistently.

PHASE

2

CREATE THE ROADMAP
AND BEGIN THE JOURNEY

CHAPTER 4

CONCEIVE

"Whatever the mind can conceive and believe, it can achieve."
—NAPOLEON HILL

Your brain is blessed with a golf ball–sized area in your frontal cortex called the lateral frontal pole. This is the part of your brain that makes you uniquely human. Its circuitry helps you make decisions, anticipate results, and plan for the future. Behavior in the animal kingdom is driven by instinct and habit; things seem to happen automatically. But *your life* doesn't just happen automatically. You are, as former President George W. Bush famously said, the decider. You have control over your actions, choices, and future. When you let your behavioral choices become instinctual rather than intentional, your life will be a struggle.

A moment of inspiration may bring a decision to pursue change, but that decision often goes unfulfilled. The reason? Because conceiving a plan to bring that decision into reality is hard work. Phase 1 of the DISCIPLINE STRATEGY (chapters 1, 2, and 3) walked you through the process of making a solid and informed decision, investigating and researching thoroughly and with an open mind, and sorting information to form a knowledge base. Now, in Phase 2 (chapters 4, 5, and 6), we turn to conceiving a plan, implementing it, and persevering through times of difficulty. Let's get started!

THE GROUND-LEVEL VIEW
(WHAT THIS LOOKS LIKE IN REAL LIFE)

Jason had made a decision to pursue his lifelong dream of becoming a country music songwriter and performer. Since age ten, he had played the guitar, performed in various bands, and even paid his way through the University of Northern Colorado School of Music, where he excelled in guitar. But after leaving college, he floundered.

Working as a waiter at one of Denver's nicer restaurants paid the bills, and Jason occasionally got a one-man gig playing guitar and cover songs at some local bars. He spent a lot of time writing songs and trying to get an audience with anyone who would listen, and he occasionally caught the eye of a music professional in Nashville. In general, though, his music career had stalled. He realized he was just another waiter with a music hobby. Something had to change.

One afternoon after several months of frustration, Jason found himself hiking up Chimney Gulch just outside Denver. He was there to get some exercise and fresh air, but he ended up getting much more than that. While gazing out over the mountain landscape, Jason had an epiphany. He felt an overwhelming emotional pull that led to a crystal-clear decision: he would commit to planting himself in the center of the country music scene in Nashville, Tennessee. He was elated. It was as if he had been waiting for this decision for years and had finally reached a now-or-never tipping point.

Jason raced back down the steep trail. He couldn't wait to get home and begin researching how he would make this major life change. For three days, he read, took notes, called people he didn't even know in the music business, and completed a self-directed cram course in becoming a Nashville songwriter. Now it was time to conceive a detailed plan to make this dream happen, but translating his enthusiasm and research into a plan of action seemed overwhelming. So he broke his challenge into chunks. He designed a phased plan that involved moving to Nashville, getting a job, joining specific writer groups, networking, visiting music venues, and more. With a plan conceived, he felt more comfortable about his decision.

THE CHALLENGES AND SOLUTIONS

The topics we covered previously—decision-making, researching, and sorting information—require knowledge and technique. Those topics can be learned and mastered. Conceiving a plan, though, is a more abstract process that can be difficult to learn simply by reading about the underlying theory. So instead of using the clear-cut challenge/solution breakdown I've used in previous chapters, I will use a detailed case study to help you understand the purpose of the plan, the challenges you will face, and the solutions that are most likely to maximize your chances for success.

This process will work for just about anything you want to accomplish in life or business. For illustrative purposes, I will introduce Amy Williams, a fictional character modeled after many of the long-distance race competitors Sandy and I know. Amy, a forty-seven-year-old nurse and mother of three, has decided to attempt a full Ironman endurance race. I'll provide more background on Amy in a moment. First, though, let's be clear about the six steps for conceiving a plan:

1. Develop a detailed roadmap using your knowledge base.
2. Create an action plan that anticipates challenges and poses solutions.
3. Establish a timeline for achieving stepping stones along the way.

4. Create an atmosphere of accountability.
5. Prepare for a mental battle by developing your "mental game."
6. Reprioritize your life and (temporarily) set aside everything that is not critical while you pursue your goal.

Now, with these steps in mind, let's see how Amy goes about conceiving her plan.

CHALLENGE: AMY WILLIAMS AND THE IRONMAN (CASE STUDY)

It had been a difficult few years for Amy. After her divorce four years earlier, she had struggled to reorganize her life, manage her finances, and coordinate her three children's many activities. John, age seventeen, was about to start his junior year of high school. He had been driving for about a year, and his mother felt comfortable with him driving himself to school. Fortunately, the middle school was located on the same campus as the high school, so John could drop off Mary and Janet, his twin sixth-grade sisters, on his way to school. This would be their first year in middle school, and the convenience of having John drop them off gave Amy some newfound freedom in her schedule.

Amy had been a nurse since graduating from Vanderbilt University's School of Nursing in Nashville twenty-six years earlier. She had worked at Vanderbilt Hospital for her entire career and had used that seniority to maintain a regular schedule, working her three required twelve-hour shifts each week on Tuesday, Wednesday, and Thursday. This gave her two weekdays to herself while the kids were at school as well as weekends to focus on the kids' extracurricular activities. It was a comfortable routine.

Now, with John picking up some of the driving duties, Amy was beginning to think about a long-forgotten dream: becoming an Ironman triathlete. This title does not come easily. As I've mentioned before, an Ironman race involves swimming 2.4 miles, biking 112 miles, and running 26.2 miles (a full marathon). And you don't get any break between events; it's a direct transition from swimming to biking to running.

Amy didn't have her first child, John, until age thirty. She fondly remembered spending her twenties being active and running various 5K races, 10K events, and several marathons. There was something uniquely rewarding about tackling these big challenges. She recalled watching, at age ten, as Julie Moss collapsed just yards from the Ironman World Championship finish line. Amy's dad enjoyed sports, and she remembered sitting beside him on their large den sofa and watching, with amazement, this crazy, exhausting race. It planted a seed that she never forgot. Just ten years old at the time, Amy had not yet bought into all the things the world tries to tell adults, such as "You can't" and "You shouldn't" and "You're not that strong." She still believed she could do *anything*—and she wanted to be an Ironman.

Sitting in church one Sunday with her three children and feeling somewhat distracted by back-to-school planning, Amy heard the minister say, "What do you want, and what are you willing to do for it?" Somehow, those words cut through the fog and stuck with her. Without even thinking, she internalized an instant response: "I want to be an Ironman." She almost blurted out loud, "I am willing to train and commit myself at whatever level I have to in order to be successful."

Amy was so excited that she could think of nothing else for the remainder of the service. Something she had thought and dreamed about for thirty-seven years and that seemed unachievable had almost miraculously come screaming into her conscious mind, and she made a commitment to pursue it.

On the way home, Amy shared with the children what she was thinking. They were all glued to their phones, catching up on everything that had happened on social media while they were at church. The twins gave a "That's cool, Mom" response and went back to texting. John, having assumed the role of the wise and prudent oldest child, asked Amy whether that was a smart thing for her to do given her age. Having learned not to immediately dismiss John's thoughtful responses, Amy told him that she would let her emotions calm down and then think some more about it.

Amy then reached out to some friends who had completed shorter swim-bike-run races called sprint triathlons. They put her in touch with Karen, a fifty-four-year-old woman who had completed a full Ironman and several half-Ironman races. Amy met with Karen, and they had a fabulous conversation. Amy quickly learned the challenges involved and the high commitment level required as Karen shared the harsh reality associated with hours-long workouts and fighting through knee and neck pain. She also described the challenges of open-water swimming, something Amy had never done, and a couple of unfortunate cycling accidents. They discussed the cost of a good road bike and the importance of a good coach. The expenses added up faster than Amy expected, but, for now, she was simply taking notes and learning about the journey to success.

The information was encouraging but also sobering. Amy left her lunch with Karen feeling more overwhelmed and scared than excited. She wasn't sure how she could afford the time or effort necessary to reach her goal. She knew she had to think through this challenge and make a decision.

Let's summarize what we can learn from this narrative so far. As is typical in most decision processes, emotions lead the way as our mind latches onto an interest or deferred ambition. That initial desire for something better is accompanied by a flood of rewarding brain chemicals. For a moment, you feel invincible! Then, as you begin to think about actually doing what you've envisioned, the slower, rational part of your mind speaks up with all the reasons why you *can't* do what you so badly *want* to do. At this stage, where Amy is now, you have to embark on the decision process as outlined in chapter 1.

Happily, Karen was one of my consulting clients and was familiar with the DISCIPLINE STRATEGY principles. She explained the decide, investigate, and sorting steps to Amy and asked if they could meet regularly so Karen could help Amy with her decision process, support her investigation into becoming an Ironman, and help her prioritize and sort her research to accommodate Amy's life situation. All this took about six weeks, after which Amy was ready to conceive her plan.

Amy learned a tremendous amount during several weeks of researching what others had done to conquer this major challenge. Her weekly meetings with Karen were valuable, too, because Karen and Amy were just a few years apart in age and had similar life situations, making Karen's firsthand stories very relevant.

Amy decided that she should train under a certified Ironman coach. She met with three coaches and selected Amanda, who had worked with over three hundred Ironman finishers and had a great record of success. Amanda had also worked with a considerable number of women in their forties who were relatively new to endurance athletics. Amy decided that her roadmap for completing the Ironman should be developed in conjunction with Amanda, but also that they should craft a plan that followed the DISCIPLINE STRATEGY suggestions.

It's worth noting here that, depending on your situation, you may want your coach, business advisor, medical consultant, or whoever may be working with you on your plan to become familiar with the DISCIPLINE STRATEGY and to support your efforts in applying this method. Having an advisor is not absolutely necessary at this point but, if you choose to have someone advising you during plan conception, try to get him or her on board with the DISCIPLINE STRATEGY.

SOLUTION: FOLLOW THE SIX STEPS OF CONCEIVING A PLAN

Now let's pull back a bit and examine how Amy utilized the six steps of conceiving a plan, which I've outlined. Remember the steps apply to *any* change process you are undertaking, so you might need to adapt the steps as needed to your specific situation.

STEP 1: DEVELOP A DETAILED ROADMAP
USING YOUR KNOWLEDGE BASE

Amy and Amanda initially took some time to synchronize their knowledge about the Ironman race. Amy had approached the topic as an outsider, researching and reading a variety of material; Amanda had been formally trained by the Ironman organization as a certified coach. Since their perspectives were quite different, they had detailed discussions to reach a common understanding. Once they had done so, Amy and Amanda designed a roadmap.

The roadmap is not a detailed step-by-step plan. Rather, it's a simple, clear, one-page document stating how you will accomplish your goal. The overall roadmap should not change throughout the process, although some of the specific procedures, habits, timing, and other parameters will be modified as you learn and grow through the accomplishment phase. The roadmap clearly states where you are going and includes a general commitment to how you will get there. This is important for three specific reasons:

1. The roadmap supports your visualization efforts. It guides you in how to visualize reaching the destination.
2. The roadmap guides your reticular activation system. It tells your brain in a very clear manner, "This is where we are going; be alert to all information that supports this goal."
3. There will be massive distractions, detours, and perhaps breakdowns throughout the journey. The roadmap is a daily reminder of where you are headed when you feel lost, confused, discouraged, and perhaps even hopeless.

Amy and Amanda decided that Amy's roadmap would consist of two things. First, she would write a document that described what she was going to do and how she would do it. This wasn't her complete action plan (that comes later). Rather, this was simply a broad one- or two-line response to the question, "How are you going to do this?" Second, she would design a vision board on which she would post her roadmap along with motivating photos and quotations. Amy knew the perfect spot for this vision board—just over her desk where she sat for thirty minutes each night to check email, pay bills, and visit social media after the children went to bed.

STEP 2: CREATE AN ACTION PLAN THAT ANTICIPATES CHALLENGES AND POSES SOLUTIONS

Amy and Amanda then developed an action plan. Any change effort will require new habits, and it can be challenging to incorporate them into your life. The action plan lays out how you will initiate these new habits, reinforce them, and overcome challenges. Amy had to fit time for swimming, biking, and running into her schedule. Amanda knew from her experiences with many athletes where and how the challenges would appear. Amy also anticipated some challenges unique to her situation. Together they addressed all of them in the action plan.

Your action plan should contain two components:

1. A *general* plan of how you will integrate new habits into your life.
2. A *specific* plan, typically constructed on a weekly basis, that tells you exactly what you will be doing and when you will be doing it.

Amy and Amanda identified the specific habits and activities she'd need to integrate into her life. Since she had Friday through Monday free each week (except for planned activities with her kids), Amy knew her longest training sessions would have to occur on those days. She couldn't imagine doing much on Tuesday, Wednesday, and Thursday, when she left for the hospital at 6:30 a.m. and returned home at 7:45 p.m. Those were already long and exhausting workdays. Amanda took time to understand the challenges that Amy had identified and then suggested this action plan:

Monday: Long bike day
Tuesday: Work; use lunchtime to attend a Pilates class
                   offered by the hospital

Wednesday: Work; training rest day

Thursday: Work; strength training in classes offered at the hospital

Friday: Long run day

Saturday: Swimming in the pool or at the lake

Sunday: Bike and run day (often referred to as a "Brick" by triathletes)

In connection with the action plan, Amy and Amanda discussed the anticipated challenges and proposed a solution for each one. Amanda explained, "In the business world, this is called a *premortem*. It's a way to anticipate what can go wrong and plan ahead of time for a resolution. It will also prevent you from adopting a 'do or die' mentality that can lead to injury."

Amy, in turn, explained that, although her four-day weekends were theoretically open, she had certain habits and routines she might find hard to give up. These included sleeping late, meeting friends for long lunches, and gardening. She wasn't sure how she would feel as her workouts grew in intensity, and she didn't want to abandon these other routines right away.

In this conversation, Amy realized for the first time that some things would have to change in order for her to accomplish her desired goal. The word *sacrifice* popped into her head again. She expressed passionately to Amanda that she didn't want to give up any of the other things she valued.

Amanda reminded her of all she would gain over the next nine months as she trained for the Ironman. First, she would gain an entirely new community of friends. While not losing her old friends (although she might not see them quite as often), she would join a new group of people committed to the same goal, people who typically formed a tight bond of camaraderie and friendship. "Amy," emphasized Amanda, "you are placing too much importance on what you currently have and what is familiar to you. You are not considering the new experiences and friend-ships that will enrich your life."

Amy acknowledged that she had been focusing heavily on what she perceived as sacrifices and that she needed to be mindful of her self-talk and pay more attention to the benefits of this new undertaking. She recognized that there could be many positive aspects of her Ironman effort that she wasn't yet seeing or considering.

So they agreed on how to deal with the perceived challenges. First, Amy would reduce spending time with old friends to make time for new training routines. The second challenge, her garden, was offloaded to a professional gardener. The third challenge was Amy's penchant for sleeping late on her days off. Amanda strongly suggested that Amy follow her workday sleep schedule—up at 5:00 a.m. and in bed at 9:30 p.m.—every day of the week while training. The more stable sleep routine, Amanda explained, would improve the quality of Amy's sleep and allow her to complete her outdoor workouts early, before it got too hot outside.

Having developed an overall action plan and anticipated the challenges with Amy, Amanda now turned to discussing the concept of *chunk it up*. She explained, "*Chunk it up* is a learning technique that can be applied to goal accomplishment and change. Instead of trying to mentally digest a massive challenge in its entirety, you chunk it up into pieces that you can manage more effectively. For you, Amy, this will be a weekly plan." Amanda was accustomed to using an online software tool called TrainingPeaks that allowed her to create a weekly training plan for Amy, to view and comment on her training data, and to make weekly adjustments based on progress.

It was now all becoming real to Amy. She sat with Amanda as they created a TrainingPeaks account, made some initial entries, calibrated the Garmin watch she would use during all workouts, and played with some test data. TrainingPeaks gave Amanda and Amy an effective way to generate a detailed action plan week by week.

Amanda added, "Don't think about how you'll complete an extra-long bike ride two months from now; you only have to do what the schedule says for the week ahead. We're building you up slowly. Your body will respond, you'll keep getting stronger, and you will be able to complete the training plan each week." These were reassuring words for Amy, who now understood that *chunking it up* had a significant psychological component to it. Amanda also suggested that Amy write the phrase, "One week at a time," on her vision board.

Any change plan will require action. In your action plan, you must see your life in its entirety as it exists today and how it must change to support your goal. Identifying new routines, habits, methods, commitments, and ways of thinking are all parts of conceiving the overall plan. This can sometimes seem deceptively easy but, when translated into a weekly plan, it can begin to appear much more daunting. The idea that "I'll take three night classes for six semesters to finish my degree" may be a plan, but when it translates into "I'll be in class on Monday, Wednesday, and Friday nights from 6:00 to 10:00 and all day on Saturday" on a weekly basis, you can see the dedication required. There is always a conceptual tension between the desire and the reality of what you need to do each week to achieve the goal. Find a balance that keeps you motivated but ensures the weekly plans make sufficient progress possible.

STEP 3: ESTABLISH A TIMELINE FOR ACHIEVING STEPPING STONES ALONG THE WAY

With the action plan complete, Amanda was ready to introduce the concept of stepping stones, or markers on the journey that let you know whether you are on course and how you are doing. Stepping stones vary based on the intended goal. I like the analogy of a pilot flying across the country. When he plans his journey, he expects to cross certain points at certain times. If these points aren't reached as expected, then he knows something is not right and reevaluates the situation. This can happen even when you think everything is going as planned. Your job is to determine appropriate stepping stones or checkpoints on the way to your goal.

Amanda and Amy agreed that the end of Amy's journey would be the September 2020 Ironman competition in Chattanooga, Tennessee. But training for that event without completing any shorter-distance triathlons would not be wise. Amanda suggested three stepping stones she felt would provide good interim checkpoints. She explained, "This will give you some practice with transitions [from swimming to biking to running] and nutrition, verify that your training is on course, and give you confidence that you can succeed." Amy understood the need for training races, but she had not recognized their full benefit as checkpoints, giving her a way to measure her progress and evaluate her training plan at key points in her training. Together, Amy and Amanda chose three stepping stones:

March 2020: Sprint triathlon
May 2020:   Olympic distance triathlon
July 2020:   Half-Ironman

Amanda explained that these stepping stones would be used to assess Amy's training progress and identify any difficulties so they could make necessary adjustments to her plan. The stepping stones would also allow Amy to observe her own progress and build confidence—two critical goals at this stage.

Design your stepping stones to make sure you are on course, but also use them to note and celebrate your progress. Your change journey may be a long one, and it is important to notice and be encouraged by the progress you are making along the way.

STEP 4: CREATE AN ATMOSPHERE OF ACCOUNTABILITY

One of the most powerful parts of your plan is accountability, which can be achieved through three steps:

1. Make a public declaration concerning your goal and your progress toward that goal.
2. Establish a regularly scheduled dialogue with a friend, mentor, advisor, or coach.

3. Review on a regular basis your stated goal, lessons learned, and decisions made.

Amanda discussed at length with Amy the psychological challenges she would face as her training grew in length and intensity. There would be difficult days when Amy would question what she was doing, and Amanda knew from experience that public and personal accountability commitments can often be crucial in getting through the difficult times.

Amy had long enjoyed following her friends and sharing some of her special life moments on Facebook. She was planning to reduce the time she spent on Facebook during her training months, but Amanda suggested she still take the time to create a sense of Facebook-based public accountability concerning her training. By sharing what she was doing, including the successes and challenges, she would receive some motivational benefit from the social pressure that such a public announcement can create.

Amanda suggested next that Amy find a friend or fellow triathlete to meet with every few weeks to discuss their training. Amy had recently met Denise, about ten years her junior, at a cycling clinic, and they had quickly become friends. Denise was also preparing to train for the Chattanooga Ironman in 2020, and Amy thought she might be the perfect accountability partner. Amy reached out to Denise and suggested that they plan a regular luncheon date every three weeks to compare notes, encourage each other, and, most importantly, hold each other accountable.

Finally, Amanda didn't want the budding triathlete to miss or forget any valuable lessons during the hectic weeks ahead, so she outlined the concept of a *lessons-learned document* and instructed Amy to create one on her computer. In this document, she would begin recording what she was learning and deciding during her journey.

Amanda gave some examples. "If you decide to vary from the sleep schedule we put together and find that you feel less productive and effective as a result, you could write in your lessons-learned document, 'My sleep schedule serves me well, and I will not vary from it. For a couple of days during the third week in March, I decided to sleep late on my days off. This put me behind on my training schedule, and I felt rushed and even had a mild headache.' " Amanda acknowledged that it may seem unusual to keep notes like this, but she had found that it provides a powerful way to document, remember, and reinforce what was being learned. Amanda told Amy, "I will put a reminder in your TrainingPeaks plan each week for you to review your lessons-learned document. This mental training is just as important as your physical training. You must capture and cement in your mind the lessons you learn through this journey."

STEP 5: PREPARE FOR A MENTAL BATTLE BY DEVELOPING YOUR "MENTAL GAME"

Early in Amy's training, Amanda scheduled a two-hour walk for them at a nearby park. She had found the psychological aspects of plan conception were best contemplated while moving, walking, and reflecting. "There will be some challenging workouts in the weeks and months ahead, but I won't ask you to do anything you aren't ready to do," Amanda emphasized. "You will be *physically* strong, but you will also need to develop *mental toughness.*"

Amy worried that this mental part could actually be more difficult than the physical aspects of training for an Ironman. Her life was busy, and her job was often emotionally draining. As a single mother of three kids, she had the potential for an unexpected life challenge or emotional upheaval at any time. Mental-toughness training would be just as critical as checking off all the workouts that Amanda loaded into TrainingPeaks each week.

Mental-toughness training is not an exact science, but there exists an agreed-upon set of strategies that experts from diverse fields like military training and sports psychology use effectively. These techniques and concepts can be applied in a variety of situations. Amanda outlined the following mental-toughness training for Amy:

1. **Learn to meditate.** Meditation has been shown to improve performance in a variety of circumstances. Amanda shared her own experience with the Headspace app, which is a quick and effective way to begin meditating.

2. **Practice "square breathing."** Square breathing is used to calm the mind and overcome fears. To do this, inhale for a count of four, hold the breath for four seconds, exhale for a count of four, and then hold the exhale for a count of four. Do this ten times each day.

3. **Become an imaginer.** Disney popularized the term "imagineering," but the concept works well for turning visualization into a much richer, all-senses experience. Amanda explained, "Amy, I want you to mentally rehearse each workout with every sense and with positive emotion. This can be done early in the morning after your meditation time. Also, each night before you go to bed, I want you to create a fantastic movie in your head of crossing the finish line in your race and celebrating with immense joy." The mental imagineering that Amanda was suggesting appealed strongly to Amy. She had always appreciated creativity and saw this as an opportunity to use that part of her mind.

4. **Nurture psychological resilience.** Resilience is the ability to recover from negative emotional experiences. You can nurture resilience through improvements in your well-being. "I realize you may not see the connection here," Amanda told Amy, "but I want you to adopt some specific habits designed to improve your positive emotions. First, start a gratitude journal and write down several things you're grateful for each evening. Second, commit to five random acts of kindness each week. You can define what those acts are, big or small, but I want you to jot them down in your gratitude journal." Resilience is about controlling your emotional reflexes and quickly moving back to a solid base of emotional stability.

5. **Use visual cues and reminders.** "Finally," Amanda said, "we've used a couple of visual strategies with your roadmap and the visualization board that hangs over your desk. Now, I want you to take this a step further and post signs and notes that you find inspirational on your computer desktop, in your car, at work, on your bathroom mirror, and even on your body. You can use temporary tattoos with mottos that speak to you. Many of my clients do this as a fun way to add a special reminder on race day."

STEP 6: REPRIORITIZE YOUR LIFE

Amy knew the next nine months would be almost laser-focused on the most challenging thing she had ever attempted physically or mentally. During the planning process with Amanda, she had identified some of the biggest challenges to allocating the needed training time. A decision was made on how to address each issue. Amy now needed to allocate as much time as possible for this new undertaking.

STEP 2 in this chapter has already addressed obvious hurdles to implementing the training plan. This final step pushes you to open up even *more* time than you may anticipate needing. The change effort you are about to undertake, no matter what it is, will require more time and mental energy than you anticipate. But you have undertaken it because you believe the goal is significant enough to justify the sacrifices needed to get there. So, create extra room in your life for this endeavor.

In past years, Amy had occasionally taken a long weekend trip with an old college friend. They would center the trip around hiking or shopping, depending on their mood. As she and Amanda discussed reserving more time in her life for the plan they had conceived, Amy knew she'd have to push pause on these weekend trips. Late-night television, downtown concerts, and a few other activities were also suspended. "I realize this goal is going to take every bit of mental energy and commitment I can muster," Amy declared. "I am all in!"

So how did Amy do? Did she follow through with her plan, complete her training, and cross the finish line? Did she fulfill her lifelong dream of becoming an Ironman triathlete? I like to think she did. I can say that with some authority, as I've known several women and men, all with their own unique life situations like Amy, who have committed to a well-laid plan and used it to achieve what they once thought was impossible.

YOUR PLAN IS AS UNIQUE AS YOU ARE

I can give you a clear plan for the decision process, which we saw in chapter 1. I can also teach you concrete principles for conducting research and sorting information, as I did in chapters 2 and 3. Conceiving a plan, however, is different. It's much more abstract and personalized because you have to make your plan work in *your* life. What works for me may not (and probably won't) work for you. No one knows you better than you do, so it's up to you to figure out what kind of plan will make the most sense and be the most beneficial to you. Your plan will only work if you're able to follow it, so put in the work to make sure you can make your plan fit into your life.

———— TAKE IT FURTHER ————

The seeds of both success and failure are sown during your plan conception, so you've got to make your planning count. To help, check out the worksheet for this chapter at www. DISCIPLINESTRATEGY.com.

Plan Conception Worksheet

This detailed worksheet will walk you through the six steps presented in this chapter and help you develop a plan for effective change.

CHAPTER 5

IMPLEMENT

"Everyone wants to be a beast until it
is time to do what beasts do!"
—ERIC THOMAS, PH.D.

The Oxford Dictionary defines implementation as "the process of putting a decision or plan into effect; execution."[6] This is no small task. You are on a grand mission now, and your journey will require intense focus, self-control, and wisdom. The implementation phase of the DISCIPLINE STRATEGY is the point where we make the precarious transition from *planning* to *doing*. This requires a tremendous amount of dedication, willpower, and outright strength of character. As Dr. Eric Thomas says, "Everyone wants to be a beast until it is time to do what beasts do!" That's one of my favorite sayings, and I believe it beautifully summarizes the challenge of implementation. Yes, we may enjoy sitting around and planning, plotting, and preparing to be the beast. But being the beast is hard work. It requires unrelenting intensity toward

6 "Implementation," Oxford Living Dictionaries, https://en.oxforddictionar-ies.com/definition/implementation.

completing tasks and accomplishing goals. When it's time to actually do what beasts do, we discover who is truly committed. I want *you* to be committed to your dream—your life change. It is in this transition to doing where dreams become reality.

Successful implementation of your plan will depend, to a great extent, on building solid habits that support progress toward your goal. Once habits are integrated into your brain, they run in low-power mode. Forcing yourself to initiate a new or unfamiliar behavior takes tremendous willpower, and research has shown that willpower is a finite resource; eventually, we burn it up. On the other hand, the more routine habits you establish to serve your implementation plan, the more energy you will have left to face the difficult times. You want to run on autopilot as much as possible, and habits make this possible.

THE GROUND-LEVEL VIEW
(WHAT THIS LOOKS LIKE IN REAL LIFE)

Paul decided to get out of debt. The decision came after an emotional dinner with a woman he'd been dating for a couple of months. They were getting to know each other pretty well, but Paul was still going out of his way to make a good impression on her. On that fateful night, though, Paul attempted to pay for the dinner and all three of his credit cards were denied. His date picked up the tab.

She was gracious about it and really didn't think it was a big deal, but Paul was devastated. It was the moment he came face to face with the fact that, at age twenty-eight, he had more debt than he could handle. He vowed to do whatever it took to turn the financial tide.

Paul's research led him to the books and classes of personal finance expert Dave Ramsey (www.daveramsey.com). Based on what he learned, Paul conceived a plan to get out of debt in twenty-two months. His plan involved severely limiting his expenses and spending his nights and weekends working as an Uber driver to supplement his full-time salary from UPS. It would be an austere twenty-two months, to say the least.

Paul had everything laid out and scheduled, and he devoured every book Dave Ramsey had ever written. He was certainly motivated. But about a week into his new debt-elimination plan, Paul started losing interest and an unexpected opportunity taxed his limited stores of willpower. Two of his buddies were planning to attend a major-league soccer match in Atlanta the following weekend. They all but begged Paul to join them, saying they would share the ride down, split a hotel room, and buy the cheapest tickets they could find. It sounded like a fantastic weekend, and it would only cost about $200 each.

Paul knew this wasn't in his "Determined Debt-Reduction Plan." He would bust his budget by $200 *and* he wouldn't log any Uber time during the three-day trip, which would probably cost him another $150. The net impact would be a $350 loss to his get-out-of-debt plan. This was when the rubber met the road and he came face to face with how difficult the implementation stage can be.

THE CHALLENGES AND SOLUTIONS

Transitioning from *planning* to *doing* presents a unique set of challenges. The initial implementation is a high-energy step from both a physical and a mental standpoint. However, if you handle the challenges effectively and avoid the pitfalls, you can then progress to the perseverance stage, where willpower results in significant forward progress. Think of it like pushing a large piece of furniture across the room. Getting the thing moving is the hardest part. Once you overcome inertia and the piece of furniture starts to move, it requires less energy to *keep* it moving. Putting your plan into action works the same way. Implementation is a time of putting momentum behind your new habits; it takes a lot of work to get things moving, but it'll be easier once your plan is up and running—as long as you overcome the problems that will inevitably pop up.

Let's take a quick high-level look of the five main challenges you'll likely face as you work through the implementation stage:

- **STRONG INITIAL RESISTANCE:** Implementation involves switching from a goal-setting mentality to a process mentality. In other words, it marks a shift from the delirious high of *dreaming* to the daily grind of *doing*. You'll face some internal resistance here. When you first made a decision, you were selecting a goal or target for change. This focal point served you well during the following three steps: investigate, sort, and conceive. However, now your focus must be narrowed and fixed on daily task completion. To overcome the inevitable mental resistance, you will have to think in terms of baby steps, habits, and simplification.

- **STATUS-QUO BIAS:** Once you have overcome the initial resistance, your brain switches to a new tactic and the status-quo bias kicks in. This occurs when your mind tries furiously to convince you that everything really was just fine the way it was and that there is no need for change. Many believe this poses the greatest threat during the decision process, but my experience has taught me it is more likely to surface as you begin implementation. It is after you start down the new road, with all its unexpected twists and turns, that the old road begins to look extremely attractive. To win this psychological battle, you will engage with a community of like-minded people and use mental exercises to place more importance on the new life you are creating.

- **FEAR:** Fear is a powerful expression of the part of your brain called the amygdala. As you begin to *do* something, instead of just *planning* to do something, your amygdala will invoke a fear response to the unknown. This is where the dragons appear, so managing fear and anxiety is a critical skill during implementation.

- **REALISTIC EXPECTATIONS VS. PATIENCE:** One advantage of getting into your grind is that you begin to set mental expectations of daily effort as part of your system of implementation. People may tell you that you need to be patient, but patience is not what you need; rather, you need realistic time-frame expectations. We will discuss how to create and manage these appropriate expectations.
- **NOT ENJOYING THE JOURNEY:** It is easy to become fixated on the goal, but you will never reach your goal at all if you don't *enjoy* the journey. Daily recognition that you are literally becoming a different person in the process is critical to the journey's success.

With these five challenges in mind, let's take a closer look at how to confront and overcome each one by implementing a consistent set of new habits to support your DISCIPLINE STRATEGY plan.

CHALLENGE: STRONG INITIAL RESISTANCE

Implementation is all about new habits, ways of doing things, routines, and thought processes. You will feel resistance as these changes replace current habits. Thinking about starting a business and then actually waking up early to work on that business are two very different tasks. No matter what goal you are pursuing, you can anticipate resistance in some form.

SOLUTION: PUSH

Just as in moving furniture, getting past the initial resistance requires us to *push.* To keep that image front and center, here are four tips for pushing past the initial resistance, using the acronym PUSH:

- **Publicize:** First, as I discussed in the previous chapter, you need to create an atmosphere of accountability. This can be accomplished by making your new habit or routine public.

Share your commitment with friends, family members, coworkers, or on social media. Research shows we are more likely to follow through on commitments that we make publicly.

- **Usher:** Usher in your new habit by tying it to an old habit. For example, I am very committed to working out with a weight trainer four mornings a week. My consistency is high (my trainer is not someone I want to disappoint), so I can usher in a new habit of running four days a week by scheduling it right after my weightlifting. Perhaps you have a day job and you are starting a business at night to develop a new phone app, but you are having difficulty finding the time to carry out the programming work. Every day after work, you like to stop at a local coffee shop. So why not take advantage of that habit and turn it into a longer stop where you code for two or three hours? You do dozens of routine things every day; think about how you can usher in a new life routine by tacking it on to something that already works.

- **Simplify:** You must keep things simple at the beginning. Whether your goal is professional or personal, the first steps must be tiny, simple things that start you moving and give you a sense of momentum. For example, if you are returning to college to finish your degree after a ten-year hiatus, it will be best to start either by taking just a single class while you master the necessary new habits or finding an adult-degree cohort program where every step to graduation is laid out. The same is true in the business world. If you are starting a bakery, you could start with a simple product line and identify small steps for a single day at the bakery. Focus on completing those daily steps. Bakers typically start early, so if you want to be a baker, your first step might be simply mastering a 3:30 a.m. wake-up time.

- **High Five:** Give yourself a high five! At the end of my day, if I have completed my workouts, checked off my task list, and successfully pushed toward my goal, I go home and have a piece of dark chocolate and a glass of red wine. For me, that is a *huge* high five! Consciously celebrate each new habit for several days as you are locking it in place. Then, add it to your collection of habits and celebrate your progress. I'll say more about daily celebration later in this chapter.

CHALLENGE: STATUS-QUO BIAS

Despite your excellent decision-making process, which you completed in chapter 1, the day will come soon after implementation begins when your brain says, "Things really were good the way we had it. Let's just stop all this silliness and go back to the good old days." Research shows that people feel a significant desire to stick with the status quo. Our brains are structured to put more emphasis on holding on to what we have. As a result, we have a strong aversion to risking what we already have in exchange for some potential gain from a future unknown. A couple of old adages describe it best: "A bird in the hand is worth two in the bush" and "When in doubt, don't."

The decision process was designed to help you look beyond the status-quo bias, but doing that is often easier said than done. For example, if you've decided to give up a bad relationship, you might start thinking that even a bad relationship (what you know) would be better than being alone (the unknown). We've all been there; we tend to default to the status quo, holding on to what we perceive as safe and easy. This preference typically means no change and no action.

SOLUTION: AVOID COMPLEXITY AND CHOICE

Status-quo bias arises in the face of decision complexity. To avoid clinging to your old ways or old lifestyle, you must avoid turning the implementation of your plan into a complex daily decision.

In the previous chapter on plan conception, you created a vision and then broke down your action plan into smaller stepping stones of daily or weekly tasks. Now that you are implementing, you must avoid placing yourself into situations where you have to make new decisions about your plan, because this will certainly kick you into status-quo default mode and throw you off track.

For example, let's suppose you have decided to become a professional chef by attending the local culinary school. Classes meet for four hours on Saturday and three hours on Wednesday night. On three other nights each week, you have a homework assignment of preparing a certain meal and taking notes on your experience. If you wake up on Sunday morning and debate with yourself whether you should cook that night, which meal you should cook, when you should go to the grocery store, and whom you should invite to share the dinner with you, BOOM! The status quo will raise its ugly head and shut you down. You'll think, *This is way too much work. I didn't know it was going to be this hard. I should just go back to relying on Uber Eats and hanging out with my friends.*

Instead, since you already did thorough research on this culinary school during your conception phase, you should have planned a schedule that took constant decision-making out of the process. The schedule would stipulate which nights you would cook, when you'd go to the grocery store, who you'd invite to the meal, the time when you would start cooking, and any other key details that could be determined in advance.

Status-quo bias can be overcome by avoiding constant choice scenarios. Figure out how you, in your specific situation, can remove repetitive choices that aren't necessary parts of the process, and you'll greatly increase your chance for success.

CHALLENGE: FEAR

Fear is one of the strangest concepts to wrap your mind around. Even if you know there's nothing to fear, your mind and body can trick you into freaking out. Your pulse will shoot up, the hairs on the back of your neck will stand up, or you'll get a sick feeling in your stomach. It's not because you're doing something dangerous; it's because you're doing something new.

On your journey toward your goal, you will be doing new things, adopting new habits, meeting new people, going to new places, and having new experiences. All of this can evoke the fear response. However, there are some ways to lower the volume of fear—or even silence it altogether. This is a complex arena for neuroscientists, but I will share with you some straightforward approaches that will help.

SOLUTION: MINDFULNESS MEDITATION AND THE DARE RESPONSE

You need to learn two specific skills in order to control the fear and anxiety response that you may experience as you implement needed changes in pursuit of your goal. The first skill is mindfulness meditation, which will teach you how to observe and take note of your thoughts without allowing them to influence you negatively. You learn to allow them to exist, but you see them as somewhat separate from you and move on. Second, you will need to learn the DARE response to fear, which I'll unpack in a moment. Let's break these down.

MINDFULNESS MEDITATION

If you followed the previous chapter's suggestion to learn how to meditate, you already have the Headspace app and have started the introductory sessions. The most effective technique for managing fear and anxiety is mindfulness meditation. The Headspace course teaches you an effective way to learn and practice acknowledging your thoughts without letting them attract your attention. You simply note the thought as *thinking, feeling, hearing,* or some other label you consider appropriate. The process sounds simple, but it takes some practice to make this activity automatic. The Headspace app will teach you how to do this. Once you have completed the course, you should practice daily.

DARE RESPONSE

There are literally thousands of books and programs designed to help you deal with anxiety. I have digested a lot of this material over the years. The response to anxiety that I find most effective is presented in the book *DARE: The New Way to End Anxiety and Stop Panic Attacks* by Barry McDonagh. If you believe fear and anxiety pose a significant hurdle for you, explore more of what McDonagh has to offer at www.DareResponse.com.

McDonagh bases his program around the acronym DARE:

- **D**efuse It
- **A**llow It
- **R**un Toward It
- **E**ngage It

The first step is to *defuse* the situation. When you first feel anxious sensations in your body such as a fast heartbeat, sweating, nervous stomach, or racing thoughts, defuse the power of these sensations by bluntly stating to yourself, "So what?" or "Whatever." My personal response to any sense of anxiety is to smile and laugh. I have trained myself to visualize any of these feelings as a hilariously unattractive five-inch-tall creature. I metaphorically take it out of my head, set it beside me, and tell it to shut up!

Second, you must *allow* the sensation. After informing your anxiety that you really don't care about it, you must ride it like a wave in the ocean. Don't resist or fight it. This is where the meditative skills you have already acquired will be helpful. Invite anxiety to visit and sit down at the table. Note its presence ("Hmmm, that was an anxious feeling") and let it pass. If it doesn't pass, then embrace it and let it stay. McDonagh likes the phrase, "I accept and allow this anxious feeling."[7]

Alternatively, you could turn difficult memories or thoughts into funny cartoons. Sandy and I, along with two of our children, used this technique effectively after a severe car crash in which

7 Barry McDonagh, *DARE*, BMD Publishing, 2015, 54.

our vehicle was basically run over by a tanker truck. Miraculously, we walked away with only minor injuries, but we each struggled mentally and emotionally afterward as the crash replayed itself on an endless loop in our minds. I knew this emotional anguish was setting us up for some long-term trauma issues, so Sandy and I took action against it.

The four of us sat down together and discussed the technique of replacing that horrible moment with a funny cartoon. One of our children created a vision of our tiny poodle driving the tanker truck and our car comically spinning around in circles. We all came up with our own versions, and every time the mental video of the accident arose in our minds, we immediately took over as director and turned it into a hilarious movie. We were stunned by the effectiveness of this effort.

You will find many techniques managing anxiety. Some have withstood rigorous scientific testing while others have not been tested. You'll have to experiment and decide what works for you. The basic principle here is that the quickest way to dissipate anxious feelings is not to resist them but to allow them to stay and modify them into an entertaining—even funny—movie in your mind.

Third, you must *run toward* your fear. Having laughed at your anxiety and then allowing it to exist comfortably as a movie, you are ready to challenge it. Research has shown that fear and excitement have similar manifestations in our body. It is simply our *interpretation* of these physical sensations that determines whether we consider them as fearful or exciting. So take control of the situation by reframing feelings of anxiety into feelings of excitement. Tell yourself these sensations mean you are excited about what you are doing and energized by it. There is no threat. Enjoy the feelings of energy in your body.

Fourth, you must *engage* the fear. Once you have moved quickly through the preceding steps, you are ready to put your focus on something else. You have noted the feelings and labeled them. You have reframed the thoughts in a funny mental video.

And you have turned the feelings around so as to interpret them as excitement and energy. Now, move on! Turn your focus to the task at hand and prepare for what you are about to do. You have given anxiety its welcome. If it wants to stick around, that's fine. However, you have stuff to do and are therefore choosing to move on and focus intensely on the things that matter.

CHALLENGE: REALISTIC EXPECTATIONS VS. PATIENCE

"Are we there yet?" As the father of four, I have heard that question hundreds of times. As the implementor of countless plans, though, I've probably *said* it many more times than that!

To implement your plan successfully, you must acknowledge that implementation takes time—often much more time than we expect. Therefore, we must constantly examine and adjust our timeframe expectations to make sure they are realistic. The plan-conception process in the previous chapter contained components designed to help you with setting realistic expectations. You have stepping stones connected to a timeline, along with a detailed roadmap for the journey toward your goal. No amount of planning, however, will completely eliminate the impatience that will pop up at times.

SOLUTION: SHIFT TO GRIND MODE

During implementation, you shift from the cerebral exercises of thinking, deciding, researching, and planning to doing. Your brain immediately wants to know how far you have to go and how much more effort all this will take. During my own long change processes, I repeat to myself several times a day, *One day at a time!* You have a map, but your journey is long. All you have to focus on during implementation is the daily grind.

You must develop a mindset of short-term focus and a long-term vision. Your plan includes milestone goals where you will assess your progress and think about broader issues concerning your movement toward the goal. You know what your vision is;

you are probably reading it every day on your vision board. But there are only so many things you can do in a single day. Part of successful implementation involves making your daily plan and completing it. Know your grind for today, do it, and count the day a success. Then, plan for tomorrow and start over.

Impatience, of course, is the lack of *patience*, which the Oxford Dictionary defines as "the capacity to accept or tolerate delays, problems, or suffering without becoming annoyed or anxious."[8] Does that sound like you when delays and setbacks interrupt your forward progress? If not, my guess is that you didn't plan for any delays and setbacks. But—and this is crucial—they *will* happen. No plan is complete that doesn't account for roadblocks. If you understand the time frame you're working under and have realistic expectations, then impatience shouldn't be a problem.

Based on my experience with business startups, I know it can take up to five years for a business to establish itself on solid ground. Failure to understand and plan for that reality causes a lot of businesses to fail because entrepreneurs try to rush the process or throw money at the problems to make them go away faster. Sadly, that usually doesn't work; you simply can't buy your way out of every delay.

Your goal as you begin implementation is to set the expectations for one day at a time. Every evening, write down exactly what you will do the following day. Commit to it with the realization that a commitment is not conditional. Grind daily, realizing that you will raise your head at a predetermined time to gauge your progress and then return to the grind. That's how you'll win over the long haul.

8 "Patience," Oxford Living Dictionaries, https://en.oxforddictionaries.com/definition/patience.

CHALLENGE: NOT ENJOYING THE JOURNEY

"I hate this." Unfortunately, I have heard that comment from many people during the early days of implementing a plan. Having a little voice in your head screaming, "I hate this!" every three minutes will not make the journey much fun.

Enjoying the journey is both a decision and an art. Those two terms may not seem to go together, but they do. You can decide your physiological and mental posture toward your daily grind, and then you find creative ways to make it fun and reward yourself.

SOLUTION: CELEBRATE EVERY DAY

Although I have emphasized the need to develop a daily grind, I also suggest you develop a daily celebration. Enjoying the journey is about having a sense of direction and motivation every step of the way, so establish a daily, weekly, and monthly reward for completing the tasks you've set for yourself. External motivation can be great, but it relies on other people or events and may therefore never come. However, small rewards you choose for yourself and *earn* can be meaningful, motivating, and reliable because they're entirely up to you. These celebrations can be small, but they are an important part of the implementation process.

Before each day begins, you should know exactly what tasks you want to complete and have one or more goals (appropriate in size for a twenty-four-hour period) written down. At the end of the day, you should assess how you did and whether a celebration is in order. Small, day-sized celebrations might include:

BITE-SIZED VICTORIES

I keep a cookie jar on my desk with a label reading, "Today is a day worth celebrating." I see the jar every day, and it reminds me that each day is a gift and opportunity. Underneath the label, I have a brief quotation from the Vietnamese monk Thich Nhat Hanh, "Waking up this morning, I smile. Twenty-four brand-new hours are before me." At the end of a day, before I wrap everything up and plan for tomorrow, I assess how the day went. If I have accomplished what I set out to accomplish, I write a note about the day, its successes, and what was accomplished. I then deposit the note in the cookie jar. It is an act of both closure and celebration.

CHECKMARKS

As we noted in the previous chapter, one way to prepare for implementation is to clear as much distraction and unnecessary activities from your life as possible. One way I do this is with an email tickler system.[9] I batch process all my emails by storing them in daily electronic files. I check my emails a limited number of times each day and either address each message immediately upon opening it or forward it to a tickler file for a response later. Each day, I clean out the tickler file for that day. When I complete all the tasks in each day's tickler file, I put a checkmark by the day on the large, year-long calendar I keep on my desk. Research shows that the simple act of checking something off—in this case, marking the day off the calendar—is mentally and emotionally rewarding and encourages the underlying habit. In my demanding professional life, with two vibrant businesses to run and numerous other side projects, this habit has greatly improved my efficiency and productivity.

GRATITUDE JOURNAL

Gratitude supports resiliency, which in turn supports mental toughness and a positive psychological posture toward your goal. In the context of this section about enjoying the journey, the gratitude journal will help you stay focused on the positive. People often ask me what they are supposed to write in their gratitude journal or they complain that they can't think of anything to write.

9   A tickler system is a longstanding productivity tool for calendaring certain tasks and activities for certain days. A tickler file is a folder (physical or electronic) that represents a specific day. By placing an email or task in a tickler file, I am consciously deferring that action to another day. When that day comes, I will either act on the item or move it to another tickler file to address later.

This is often a sign of thinking too big. Yes, you can certainly express gratitude for your life, your loved ones, your health, and the beauty that surrounds us. But you should also use your gratitude journal as a mental reward and form of recognition.

For example, at the end of the day, express gratitude for what you were able to accomplish. Whereas I keep my jar of bite-sized victories on my desk at work, I like to keep my gratitude journal in my car. Once I arrive at home at the end of the day, I take a moment while still sitting there to write in the journal, which sits safely in the storage space between the two front seats. I park, pull out my journal, and note everything I'm grateful for from the day. This is a celebration of life, the people I work with, my family, and the fact that I went out into the world with intention and made things happen. It also allows me to put an official end to the workday. After writing in my gratitude journal, I flip a switch in my brain and enter the house in a fresh mindset.

FOOD

Rewarding yourself with food has gotten a bad reputation these days. But for some, this is an effective reward for a successful day. My reward once I return home, as I said earlier, is a glass of my favorite Kendall-Jackson red wine and a piece of dark chocolate. Occasionally, when I feel I did not live up to my expectations, I will skip the wine and chocolate. For me, the message is clear: *No celebration today. Do better tomorrow.* That is one method I use to hold myself accountable.

For you, perhaps it is a weekly meal out with friends or family to reflect on the successes of the week. Or, as a friend of mine enjoys, it is a 2:00 p.m. cup of "bulletproof coffee" that he painstakingly and lovingly prepares for himself. Don't go crazy, but experiment with something you enjoy and that has no negative health consequences.

SHARING WITH FRIENDS AND FAMILY

I usually don't talk much about my goals with friends or family; that's part of my psychological makeup. But on certain days when I feel I have achieved a grand success, I enjoy sharing with Sandy, one of my children, or a friend the specific thing that made the day unusually successful.

This can be a great celebration for truly special days but be sure to limit the frequency. Although people who care about you will enjoy hearing your success stories, talking so much about yourself on a daily basis might diminish the celebratory nature. You want this to be a special occasion, not a daily self-brag session. On really big days, talk it up; on an average kick-butt day, give your family a break and stick with your internal celebrations.

DOWNTIME

At the end of a long and successful day, some people find it rewarding to allow themselves some downtime watching television, playing video games, or engaging in some other relatively unproductive activity. Be careful, though; these activities can also be powerful distractions. To gain benefit from them, keep them as rewards granted for completing a successful day and never turn on the TV until the day's work is done.

VERBAL AND PHYSICAL CELEBRATION

Our nervous system is a fascinating part of being human. Information and stimuli flow from the nerves in our body through the spinal cord and then into the brain. Once the brain receives this information, it processes it and responds. There is therefore a two-way, wired connection between your body and your brain. When you have an awesome day, one way to celebrate is to put yourself into a positive posture such as raising your hands in victory.

This may sound uncomfortable or downright silly to you, but don't count it out just yet. You know that your physical posture affects how *others* perceive you; now, you must also understand that your posture affects how you see *yourself*. A positive pose, posture, or movement sends a strong message to your mind. Let's practice right now. Pick one of these three celebratory body movements and do it for at least thirty seconds:

- **Double Fist Pump:** This is the classic pose you see when sprinters cross the finish line with both hands raised and perhaps a repetitive pumping action of the fists for emphasis.
- **The Superhero:** Take a wide stance and place your hands or fists on your waist. Hold your head high with your chest out.
- **Jumping and Hollering:** Adding a vocal component to your celebration just feels right sometimes. On a particularly wonderful day, I like to jump up and down and whoop it up!

Celebrating may not always feel natural but give it a try regardless. Too often, we spend our days waiting for someone else to notice our daily successes, but that encouragement may never come. As a result, we can end a highly effective day with a downcast face of disappointment, feeling like the lack of attention sucked all the joy out of our success. Don't fall for this trap! If no one else is around to applaud you, learn to applaud yourself! If you killed it today, go home proud and satisfied with yourself whether anyone else noticed or not.

MAKE SUCCESS A HABIT

As I said at the beginning of this chapter, implementing your plan—no matter how well thought out and deeply researched it is—is a difficult task. It not only requires a new attitude; it requires new habits. Throughout this chapter, I've tried to give you several new habits to support your DISCIPLINE STRATEGY plan. From pushing past your initial resistance to using mindfulness meditation to overcome fear and even to making small, daily celebrations part of your normal routine, your plan depends on a new set of positive, life-affirming habits. No plan can overcome an innate unwillingness to change behaviors, so don't blame the plan if you aren't willing to change something about your life! Go back through this chapter, make a list of things to change or add to your daily grind, and get your implementation off to a great start!

———— TAKE IT FURTHER ————

There's only one recommended worksheet for this chapter but be sure to browse www.DISCIPLINESTRATEGY.com for several other additional resources to take your DISCIPLINE STRATEGY journey even further.

Daily Journal Page

Use the DISCIPLINE STRATEGY Daily Journal page (also used in chapter 1) to capture the specifics of your daily grind. This should include reminders of your new end-of-day habits like recording your bite-sized victories, recording thoughts in your gratitude journal, and any other daily celebrations. The Daily Journal is designed with room for you to customize it for your specific purposes.

CHAPTER 6

PERSEVERE

"Obstacles can't stop you. Problems can't stop you. Most of all, other people can't stop you. Only you can stop you."
—Jeffrey Gitomer

When I started my first business in 1991 to develop niche software products, I set up a small office in the bonus room of our home and hung a framed poster on the wall. The poster showed a man running by himself on an open road. Below the image it read, "Perseverance: On the road to success, there is never a crowd on the extra mile."

Perseverance resonated with me early in life. I readily bought into the concept that perseverance would result in success, but I did not anticipate just how often I would encounter obstacles that would require perseverance. So far in this book, I have said little about my own life; in this chapter, however, I will share some recollections from my own journey when perseverance was critical.

In January 1990, at age twenty-six, I had a corporate job as a consultant and new-product developer at a large financial services firm. One day, I began thinking about how to convert the mainframe computer models I had developed into PC-based software programs. I knew the demand for such software would be strong. If you are younger than forty, it may be difficult to recall what a PC was like in 1990. Computers were just starting to appear throughout small and large businesses, and there was a significant need for software to make these devices useful. I took my idea for a suite of PC-based software tools to my boss, who promptly dismissed the concept as completely implausible. I had walked in with visions of being tapped to lead the new corporate division that would develop and market PC-based software. Instead, I walked out of his office feeling disappointed and, to be honest, confused. It had seemed like such a fantastic opportunity to me.

Around that time, I discovered at my local library a set of six cassette tapes by Earl Nightingale called *The Strangest Secret*. These tapes were my first course on success, motivation, and perseverance. While listening to them, I latched onto the belief that if I created a vision for a startup software company, launched the business, and never gave up, I could craft my own success story. From that point on, I had a very high level of determination. Looking back at the obstacles I faced, I don't think I could have been successful without that dogged determination to never give up.

When I started my business in 1990, Sandy and I had one child, another one on the way, a new home, two cars, and limited cash flow. I couldn't even afford to buy a computer to use for programming my software! Instead, I got a friend to borrow the "floater" laptop from his workplace and let me use it during off hours—typically between 9:00 p.m. and 1:00 a.m. I maintained this routine for five years before reaching the point where I could quit my day job.

Soon after completing my first software program, I switched corporate jobs and quickly discovered my new position was much more demanding than the previous one. At the same time, my software business started generating tech support calls that came in to the answering machine at my home office. I couldn't return calls from my corporate office because most of them were long distance (yes, this was a huge consideration before the spread of cell phones and national calling plans), and I certainly wasn't going to do anything to jeopardize my day job. As a result, I spent my lunch hour calling customers from a pay phone at the Marriott hotel down the street. Without a computer in front of me, I had to visualize the customers' software issues in my head and walk them through resolving their problems. Based on some of the strange looks I got from the Marriott guests, the conversations must have sounded quite odd at times.

I slowly made progress, selling one software license at a time using direct mail and stuffing envelopes into the late hours of the night. The support requirements continued to grow and began to push the boundaries of what I could handle by myself. By this point, our third child was on the way and it proved to be an extremely difficult pregnancy. Sandy had to stop working to deal with some significant health issues. As a result, I found myself working hard to meet the demands of my corporate job during the day and then rushing home to help Sandy and our two young children. For a while, all my software coding took place in the back seat of my car during my lunch hour. I'd be crammed in there frantically trying to code in one-hour blocks while my work colleagues were relaxing at a local restaurant. It was crazy for a while, but Sandy, our newborn son, our older two children, and I all managed to survive ... somehow.

As the business continued to grow, it became difficult to manage my day job, the software business, and my home life all at once. With three kids, it now made sense—from a financial and family well-being standpoint—for Sandy to be at home full time. I began to supplement our income with a monthly draw from the software business—something I'd avoided up to this point. This strategy worked for a while and helped us through some tough times, but the business soon ran out of cash. Reluctant to pump personal funds from our home checking account into the business, I decided to keep it afloat with credit cards (not recommended), but more alarming was the fact that I could see the business plateauing.

I had to make a decision: either close the business or quit my day job so I could dedicate my full attention to turning my five-year-old software company into a long-term, sustainable, and growing business. I ultimately resigned from my corporate job, much to the dismay of my boss, whom I greatly admired and who had assured me that my future within the organization was bright. But I had committed to focusing all my professional efforts on my software business and moving forward with certainty.

Literally the day I resigned from my job, I arrived home to find a legal notice advising me to cease and desist from all business activities or face legal ramifications. My software utilized a public database of information gathered and published by a large nonprofit organization, and I had obtained verbal permission from the organization a few years earlier to utilize these data. Now, however, the nonprofit was becoming a for-profit entity and viewed me as a competitor. That was laughable, but it didn't matter. Mere hours after leaving my "safe and secure" corporate career, I was staring at a letter that effectively shut down my business. The timing was stunning, even theatrical.

It would have been easy to crawl back to the corporate office with my tail between my legs and beg for my old job back. Believe me, it was tempting. But I made a different choice. I chose perseverance. The decision to proceed had been made, and I never looked back. I found a couple of great business advisors and a strong lawyer, achieved an acceptable resolution to the cease-and-desist issue, and was able to proceed with building my business.

Throughout twenty years of growing my software company, dozens of additional obstacles easily could have crushed the business or thrown it off course. You, too, will face some daunting obstacles. There is only one way to overcome them and stay fully focused on your goal with a level of complete commitment that may seem unreasonable to those around you. The answer is perseverance.

Perseverance is a decision you must make early on and one that affirms the following commitments with no doubt, hesitation, or uncertainty:

1. I will never give up.
2. I may change course, revamp my plan, or learn from my mistakes, but I *will* reach my destination.
3. I will view every hurdle as an opportunity, every challenge as a chance to grow, and every setback as a time to reassess before pushing harder than ever.
4. What matters most is that I grind away daily, every day, without end or exception, until I reach my goal.

Perseverance will take you further than practically anything else. It's the rocket fuel that will propel you toward your ultimate goal. As author Jeffrey Gitomer says, "Obstacles can't stop you. Problems can't stop you. Most of all, other people can't stop you. Only you can stop you." Perseverance will keep that from ever happening.

THE GROUND-LEVEL VIEW
(WHAT THIS LOOKS LIKE IN REAL LIFE)

Marsha knew this day would come. She started her business, a small French eatery in the trendy part of Austin, Texas, thirteen months ago. She worked and saved for six years to fund the startup. She studied culinary techniques with two great chefs during her summers in college. Marsha had practiced and honed her skills, and starting her restaurant was a dream come true. She spent more than two years deciding on the best location and the exact menu to offer, and she even made a significant investment in becoming a certified sommelier.

Despite receiving excellent reviews from food critics and great customer comments on social media, and despite knowing the metrics of her business by memory, Marsha could not ignore one critical fact: she was out of cash. She remembered one of her business professors in college who stressed, "The only reason any business fails is that it runs out of cash." Panic coursed through her body. She knew she was not prepared for this moment—the test of facing failure.

A quotation that a good friend had given Marsha when she opened her business sat in a small frame on her desk. She had never really paid much attention to it, but now it caught her eye. It said, "I'm convinced that about half of what separates the successful entrepreneurs from the unsuccessful ones is pure perseverance." She had a decision to make that would shape the course of her life.

THE CHALLENGES AND SOLUTIONS

Plenty of books and research papers have been written about perseverance. One popular reframing of the topic, published by Angela Duckworth, is the book *Grit: The Power of Passion and Perseverance.* There, she argues that grit—a popular buzzword in modern self-help circles—is made up of two key ingredients: perseverance and continuity of interest. As a researcher and as an entrepreneur, I have found the true value of *grit* comes primarily from perseverance. Therefore, we will stick with this word rather than the more popular *grit* to describe your unwavering commitment to your goals.

Many other books have discussed why perseverance matters, what personality traits correlate with perseverance, and how we might train people to have more perseverance, but I have found no book that addresses what you need to do *right now.* Too often, perseverance is discussed as theory, something to understand and appreciate. But it isn't merely a theory; perseverance is action! You must understand how to leverage the perseverance you have, magnify it, and utilize it to push through the challenges you are about to face. If you are reading the DISCIPLINE STRATEGY in its entirety before you start your change process, there is time to bump up your perseverance. If you are already underway, then focus on magnifying what you have.

As I've walked people through the DISCIPLINE STRATEGY process, I've identified four common challenges in the area of perseverance. They are a lack of:

- **PSYCHOLOGICAL CAPITAL:** Insufficient psychological capital (or PsyCap, as it is often abbreviated) can quickly pull the rug out from under you when perseverance is badly needed. PsyCap describes your mental posture toward your specific goal, your life, and the world in general. During tough times, your PsyCap level will impact any performance related to goal achievement. We will discuss an exercise to help you increase your PsyCap.

- **MENTAL TOUGHNESS:** Mental toughness, which we touched on in chapter 4, must be an essential part of any plan. Lack of mental fortitude will prevent you from pressing on in the face of a major obstacle or frustration. Fortunately, we can apply research and experience from sports psychology, the military, and martial arts to help us understand what mental toughness is.

- **PHYSICAL STRENGTH:** Perseverance often means long hours of work, stress, and high cortisol levels. Physical weakness will be like an anchor tied around your neck during these times. To help avoid this, we will discuss a specific action plan for improving your physical strength.

- **WILLPOWER:** As I have mentioned several times throughout *Discipline Strategy*, willpower is an exhaustible resource and you don't want to waste it. You will need as much willpower as you can muster to amplify your perseverance when needed, so we'll discuss how to avoid the willpower drought.

With these four pitfalls in mind, let's dig into each one to better understand the problems and identify solutions for leveraging and magnifying your perseverance.

CHALLENGE: LACK OF PSYCHOLOGICAL CAPITAL

Psychological capital, according to Dr. Fred Luthans, can be summed up as the mental posture you take toward the world.[10] It has four dimensions:

1. **HOPE:** This means having the willpower (which we will discuss in a moment) and seeing the path (that is, your action plan) to reach your goal. Realizing there is more than one way to reach your goal increases hope and psychological capital.

2. **EFFICACY:** Also referred to as self-efficacy or confidence, efficacy has been defined by prominent psychologist Albert Bandura as belief in one's ability to succeed in specific situations or accomplish a task.[11] When your efficacy is high, you have the confidence that sustains your energy and desire to tackle a challenging task.

3. **RESILIENCY:** This is the capacity to recover quickly or bounce back from adversity, setbacks, and challenges. In the context of PsyCap, resiliency is the ability to do better than just bounce back. It means the ability to respond in a way that moves you well beyond the obstacle and builds inner strength.

4. **OPTIMISM:** This is the most debated and often misinterpreted dimension of PsyCap. It is not a rose-colored view of the world but a mentally healthy way to address events in your life. As an optimist, you recognize which external events you can control, understand your personal characteristics that contribute to success, and view the future with realism and flexibility.

10 Fred Luthans, Kyle W. Luthans, and Brett C. Luthans, "Positive psychological capital: Beyond human and social capital," University of Nebraska–Lincoln, 2004.

11 Albert Bandura, "Self-Efficacy" in V. S. Ramachaudran (Ed.), *Encyclopedia of Human Behavior*, Volume 4, Academic Press, 1994, 71-81.

You may have noticed that the first letters of each of those dimensions spell the word *HERO*. That was not Dr. Luthans's intention, but it serves as an appropriate acronym. You need to nurture your HERO within to power your perseverance.

It can be difficult to objectively measure your stores of psychological capital without some help. Fortunately, I've developed a comprehensive tool that can quickly and accurately measure your PsyCap and several other personality and psychological traits. If you haven't yet taken the MyPersonality Assessment, I suggest you stop and do it right now. It will only take ten or fifteen minutes, but it will bring an entirely new perspective on everything we're discussing in this book. You can take the assessment for free at www.DISCIPLINESTRATEGY.com using the code **85285**.

SOLUTION: AN EXERCISE FOR INCREASING PSYCHOLOGICAL CAPITAL

Some organizations and researchers have designed successful exercises to increase PsyCap in a work setting. Given the broad applicability of the DISCIPLINE STRATEGY, I have designed a more general approach you can use to improve your PsyCap and support your life-change effort. This exercise is captured in the Obstacles and Perseverance Worksheet available at www. DISCIPLINESTRATEGY.com. Here's a breakdown of the steps in this process, which you'll find on the worksheet:

STEP 1: REFRAME AND REASSESS THE CHALLENGE
When you encounter a significant challenge that may require perseverance, your first step is to move past your emotional response and logically define and reframe the challenge. In this first step, write a brief summary of the challenge as you initially perceived it. Next, write a more positive summary of the challenge.

STEP 2: TAKE STOCK OF RESOURCES
In this second step, take a moment to think of all the resources that may be available to help you navigate the challenge. They

may include time, money, people, and knowledge. You may need to expand the scope of your perception. What are you not considering? What available assets have you not noticed previously?

STEP 3: UNDERSTAND AND TAKE CONTROL OF YOUR WORLDVIEW

Your explanatory style, a concept introduced by Dr. Martin Seligman, influences how you interpret things that happen and how you anticipate and plan for the future.[12] It determines whether you are optimistic or pessimistic. When something bad happens, the optimist says, "This is a temporary setback. It is not permanent, and there was some external cause that is temporary. In general, I expect success and know I can find a way to move forward or around this obstacle." The pessimist, on the other hand, says, "This is just how things are going to be. Nothing ever works out for me. There is nothing I can do about this."

Obviously, you want to foster an optimistic view of your situation by seeing the challenge through the following prism:

- This problem or challenge does not reflect my intentions and is an unexpected event I did not cause. This is just one of those random life events—bad luck, if you will—and I am confident that I can choose a positive response.
- This problem or challenge is not a permanent and unchangeable situation. This is not the norm.
- What does this realistically affect in my life? I will not blow it up to be something bigger than the temporary problem or challenge that it is. This does not forecast anything about the future or set a precedent. It is a one-time event that I will overcome. I will respond appropriately and adjust.

12 G.M. Buchanan, M.E. Seligman, and M. Seligman, *Explanatory Style*, Routledge, 2013.

STEP 4: SET A SUB-GOAL DESIGNED TO
ADDRESS THIS PROBLEM OR CHALLENGE

Perseverance emerges from focus, intention, and resources. To direct these, you need a goal. Obviously, you have an overriding goal based on your decision at the beginning of the DISCIPLINE STRATEGY process. This new sub-goal will function within the larger goal to solve the immediate situation. Take the following steps as outlined on the worksheet:

1. Write a clear, measurable goal that will move you past the problem or challenge.
2. Consider the resources outlined in STEP 2 above to form several routes to achieving your goal.
3. Draw a logic diagram or picture of the different routes to your goal. When you plot driving directions on Google Maps, you see multiple routes offered to you. In the same way, you want to generate multiple routes around your obstacle. This helps increase the hope component of PsyCap. Hope is driven by awareness of different paths to get to where you are going.
4. Finally, at the bottom of the worksheet, set a time frame for when you intend to put this problem or obstacle behind you. Recognize that perseverance may need to be accompanied by an increase in time and intensity to overcome this challenge.

I've used this exercise with hundreds of friends, colleagues, and clients, and I've found that the people who take it seriously and make an honest effort to increase their psychological capital find great success with the Obstacles and Perseverance Worksheet. Check it out at www.DISCIPLINESTRATEGY.com.

CHALLENGE: LACK OF MENTAL TOUGHNESS

Mental toughness is the intersection of many of the concepts we have discussed so far. It combines personal strength, a positive outlook, excellent habits, and an awareness of focus and goals. Specialized training in this area has garnered a lot of attention during the past decade. This emphasis emerged from sports, the military, and martial arts, but it applies to any life situation that requires perseverance. In fact, several studies have found a direct correlation between mental toughness and behavioral perseverance. More battles than you'd think are won or lost in the mind, so let's make sure you've got your head on straight.

SOLUTION: FOLLOW THE DISCIPLINE STRATEGY

Mental toughness should emerge naturally when you apply what you have learned in the DISCIPLINE STRATEGY. It's such a key piece of the DISCIPLINE STRATEGY puzzle that I included it in the MyPersonality Assessment. If you're curious about your potential for mental toughness and you haven't done the assessment yet, check it out for free at www.DISCIPLINESTRATEGY. com using the code **85285**.

Mental toughness, as generally accepted within the research community, is composed of motivation, self-confidence, attentional focus, and coping with pressure.[13] The diagram below shows how the many skills developed by following the DISCIPLINE STRATEGY support your mental toughness.

Mental toughness is about having the physical and mental strength to put yourself in the game, to actually make the decision and follow through with the plan. Yes, it is a choice. It is a choice to overcome resistance and to realize that what you are doing is not going to kill you but, rather, build you into the type of person that can accomplish the goal you have set for yourself. But the choice to be mentally tough is facilitated by the four pillars shown in the diagram: motivation, self-confidence, attentional focus, and coping with pressure. As you are reading through this book, do

---

13 Daniel F. Gucciardi1, Sheldon Hanton, Sandy Gordon, Clifford J. Mallett and Philip Temby, "The Concept of Mental Toughness: Tests of Dimensionality, Nomological Network, and Traitness," *Journal of Personality*, 83(1), 26–44.

Mental Toughness

MOTIVATION	SELF-CONFIDENCE	ATTENTION FOCUS	COPING WITH PRESSURE
Goal Setting	Baby Steps	Meditation and Mindfulness	D.A.R.E. Response
Visualization	Celebrate Success	Task List	Meditation and Mindfulness
Build Intrinsic Motivation	Build PsyCap	Vision Board	View Anxiety as Positive
Stepping Stones	Modeling/Learning from Mentors	Action Plan	Cognitive Restructuring
Physical Strength	Bite-Sized Successes		· Identify negative thoughts
Nurtured Health & Wellness	Recall Positive Performance		· Use thought stopping cue
			· Replace negative thought with positive thought

you dismiss the advice to get in the best shape of your life, discipline your mind, establish a variety of healthy habits, clear out the junk from your life, and the other suggestions that you don't think are relevant? Then I am telling you that your mental toughness will not be there when you need it—and you *will* need it.

If you were to think of someone who is mentally tough, you might imagine someone like a Navy SEAL and think, *I'm just not that type of person.* A Navy SEAL is an extreme example of mental toughness and that is the result of some very long and brutally intense training. I'm not suggesting that you must rise to that level. But I am suggesting, and strongly encouraging, that you create a level of mental toughness that far exceeds what you have demonstrated in the past. This is achieved by focusing on all the pillars that facilitate your mental toughness.

CHALLENGE: LACK OF PHYSICAL STRENGTH

A lack of physical well-being, especially cardiological and respiratory weakness, can have a dramatic impact on your perseverance. This has been shown in a variety of research studies and intuitively makes sense.

When I was a Navy ROTC midshipman at Vanderbilt University in 1981, I recall a 4:00 a.m. run through Nashville's Centennial Park that included a 4:30 a.m. mid-run lecture break. In that early morning lecture, a Marine Corps captain addressed us from the bow of an ornamental cement ship. His words had a dramatic impact on me. He emphasized the potential trials that awaited us as military officers and the critical need for a high level of personal fitness to support the effort required in those moments. Perhaps it was the setting or slightly delirious state of my brain in the pre-dawn hour, but I became a believer. Little did I know that lecture would serve me well in the years ahead—not as a Navy aviator (perseverance met its limits when my poor color vision cut short my military aspirations) but instead as an entrepreneur.

Serious challenges require not only perseverance and a positive mindset but also pure physical energy. Although there is no instant fix for physical weakness, you can achieve significant improvement by committing to an easy-to-implement plan for improving your physical strength.

SOLUTION: COMMIT TO PROPER NUTRITION AND BUILDING STRENGTH

There are thousands of books on strength, health, and well-being. Improving your physical strength isn't complicated, but it certainly isn't easy. The biggest challenge is to build sufficient internal motivation to do what must be done. Below, I summarize a step-by-step plan for improving your strength, which will result in improved ability to persevere. I assume you have the needed intrinsic motivation; otherwise you wouldn't have made it this far in the DISCIPLINE STRATEGY. If your goal is important enough to you, you shouldn't hesitate to implement key lifestyle changes that will supercharge your capacity for perseverance. Now get to work! You can (and should) implement all these steps *today*.

STEP 1: PURGE YOUR HOME AND OFFICE OF ALL JUNK FOOD

This includes anything that is highly processed or contains added sugar. Get a large trash bag and throw the stuff away!

STEP 2: EAT HEALTHY FOOD

If you have already come to a well-informed, well-researched decision about what a healthy diet means for you, follow that way of eating with very few exceptions. I'll caution you, however, not to *assume* you know what "healthy" looks like. The road to obesity is paved with good intentions and bad information. If you're just beginning your research and need a dietary plan, I suggest you check out Dr. William Davis's helpful guidelines on his website, www.wheatbellyblog.com, and in his number-one bestselling book, *Wheat Belly: Lose the Wheat, Lose the Weight, and Find Your Path Back to Health*.

I know dietary guidelines are the subject of great debate and even the USDA recommended diet has come under fierce scrutiny in recent years. I'm not saying you *have* to follow Dr. Davis's specific plan in order to be healthy; I will say, though, that this is the plan that has worked best for me. Whatever path you choose, make sure it's covered in respected, reliable research—and then stick with it.

STEP 3: LIFT SOMETHING HEAVY

Undertake resistance training to protect joints, build muscle strength, avoid injury, increase metabolism, and maintain longer periods of focus during work sessions. In this regard, I suggest three options:

    1. Hire a weight trainer. This is the quickest way to train consistently and safely with weights or resistance. It can be pricey, but it's worth it if you can afford it and stay committed.

2. Join a fitness facility. The failure rate here is high because many people join and then never go. But that's not you, right? Join a local gym or YMCA and commit to at least two days per week—one upper-body and one lower-body routine. Keep it simple. If possible, you should meet with a staff fitness trainer once or twice at the beginning to establish a routine; then, update it once every ninety days by scheduling another session with a trainer.

3. Create a workout program from YouTube videos, body-weight exercises, and fitness bands. By combining these resources, you can assemble an inexpensive program you can do at home. I won't recommend any specific YouTube videos; just search for something you like and stick to it. It doesn't have to be perfect. Then, switch it every ninety days to keep the workouts fresh and to continually push your body further.

STEP 4: GET MOVING

The simplest way to boost your general fitness is to walk one hour per day. Even thirty minutes or so will make a significant contribution to your health. The next step up is to elevate your heart rate by jogging, cycling, sprinting, or swimming. This is not a fitness book, so I'll limit my specific suggestions here and trust you to apply the research techniques from chapter 2 to your physical fitness plan. I can, however, give you two helpful tips that have served me well:

1. Buy a fitness tracker or smart watch and track your daily number of steps. Aim to walk at least 10,000 steps per day.

2. Push your heart with short, intense bursts of effort by incorporating sprints into your cardio routine. If you ride a stationary bike, for example, add a few thirty-second sprints of all-out effort into your workout. Learn more about this highly effective method by researching "sprint workouts" or "HIIT (high intensity interval training) workouts."

You may argue, "Tim, I hate working out. I don't have time to work out. I don't have the equipment I need to work out." On and on the list of the excuses goes. Let's get real for a minute. The decision you made at the beginning of this process should be so important to you that you'll do practically anything to achieve your goal. I'm speaking from experience here: your health (or lack thereof) will impact your goals and your ability to *achieve* those goals more than anything else. If you're serious about the decision you've made and the plan you've conceived, you *must* accept the supporting decision to be fit, healthy, and strong. Don't wimp out on this. I know you're stronger than that.

CHALLENGE: LACK OF WILLPOWER

I have mentioned several times throughout the DISCIPLINE STRATEGY that willpower is a finite resource. In their book, *Willpower*, Roy Baumeister and John Tierney present a compelling argument that willpower is a finite resource that is depleted as you use it. To persevere, you need to draw on your willpower. If it has been depleted by things in your life that are unrelated to your goal, you will struggle when perseverance is required, because these various life tasks are all drawing from that one reservoir. Not only is willpower required to fuel perseverance, but lack of willpower will magnify unpleasant emotions, increase tendencies toward poor habits, and intensify undesirable cravings.

SOLUTION: FILL THE RESERVOIR AND DRAIN IT SLOWLY

From my early years as a mechanical engineering student, I recall the classic introductory engineering problem in which a bucket is being filled with water at a certain rate while water is removed from it at a different rate. The same applies to managing your willpower reservoir. It can be deceptively hard to manage this process, but it is critical for the fill rate to stay ahead of the drain rate or you will find you have no ability to persevere.

EAT RIGHT, BE FIT, SLEEP SOUNDLY

To fill your willpower reservoir, you must nurture the healthy habits of eating right, exercising, and getting enough sleep. In fact, one research study found physical fitness was a strong predictor of willpower and self-control at work.[14]

I have already provided some suggestions for both fitness and diet. To use those strategies to improve willpower, you must make them an automatic part of your lifestyle. The decision to eat right and exercise cannot be something you reassess each day. Make the decision once and for all and avoid the temptation to *unmake* and *remake* the decision each day. Structuring your life routines around this decision makes eating healthy and working out automatic, requiring no willpower expenditure and instead filling up your reservoir every day that you follow the plan.

Poor sleep hygiene will also wreck your health and suck your stores of willpower completely dry. Furthermore, lack of sleep will lead to stress and an unhealthy, potentially depressed, outlook on life. If you struggle to sleep well, you will have to find your own customized answer. Whereas solutions to diet and fitness challenges can be written in a few paragraphs and are widely applicable, sleep issues are much more iterative. You'll have to conduct your own research (we discussed research techniques in chapters 2 and 3) and experiment to see what works best for you. This isn't an area you should ignore; it merits a significant effort to fix any sleep problems and support your perseverance reservoir. If you simply don't know where to start, talk to your doctor. A primary care doctor or, even better, an ENT (ear, nose, and throat) doctor will have a wealth of information and options for you.

SIMPLIFY YOUR LIFE

In 2014, a small book by Marie Kondo titled *The Life-Changing Magic of Tidying Up* became a worldwide bestseller. Then, in

14 K.H. Schmidt, R. Beck, W. Rivkin, and S. Diestel, "Self-Control Demands at Work and Psychological Strain: The Moderating Role of Physical Fitness," *International Journal of Stress Management*, 23(3), 255.

2019, everyone I know started talking about Kondo's immensely popular Netflix series, *Tidying Up with Marie Kondo*. Why would a book about organizing your life become so popular? Why would families crowd around their televisions to watch an eight-part series about cleaning up their homes? Because it resonates with our deep need to remove clutter from our lives, both physically (in our surroundings) and cognitively (in our minds). You may not realize it, but every piece of *something* in your life takes up space in the real world (your home, office, and so forth) *and* in your mind. Ownership is a wonderful thing, but it carries with it certain responsibilities. So the more stuff you have, the more responsibilities you have.

By tidying up, you simplify your life. In doing so, you decrease mental nagging about things left undone, strip away the useless junk that surrounds your home and office, free your mind of the unnecessary responsibilities that come with a garage full of stuff, and, in turn, reduce the constant drain on your willpower. The overall goal of tidying is to live in an organized manner and surround yourself with a few things that bring you joy. This reorganization of your environment can contribute significantly to your ability to persevere during a difficult time. So, get at it!

I was a big fan of simplification long before Kondo made it cool. After years of trial and error, here are the top ten simplification practices I've found most useful:

1. Say no. Right now, you are focused on a major goal and life-change effort. Say no to anything that is not in direct support of that effort.

2. Limit chat. Instant messaging, emails, and phone calls may serve as interruptions that complicate your life. You are on a mission, so stay focused and limit your distractions. Set aside a certain time of the day for non-critical communication.

3. Wake up at the same time every day. This simplifies your life by keeping daily routines on the same schedule.

4. Batch-process food preparation. Plan and prepare your meals for the week in advance. Dedicate Saturday or Sunday

to meal prep, cook in large quantities, and freeze meals to enjoy during the week.

5. Simplify getting dressed. Decide on a routine that simplifies dressing decisions on a daily basis.

6. Subcontract chores. A great number of personal service providers, often accessible through well-designed apps, allow you to hire people for just about any chores you may have. Utilize these services to reduce your workload and further simplify your planning.

7. Design each day with intention. Spend a few minutes at the end of each day or at the start of each morning writing a list of tasks for that day with a focus on your goal.

8. Give up or greatly reduce media consumption. Americans watch, on average, more than seven hours and fifty minutes of television per household per day, according to *The Atlantic*.[15] That blows my mind! I don't care what your goals are, there's no way you can waste several hours a day on TV and still accomplish what you've set out to do. Turn it off!

9. Focus on one thing at a time. Research clearly shows that we can't effectively multitask. Focus on one thing at a time; then, move to the next thing. Develop your daily task list with this fact in mind.

10. Don't buy new stuff. Stop buying anything other than necessities for a set period, such as three months. Shopping, purchasing, integrating the additional items into your life, dealing with new-product issues—all this takes time and distracts you from your goal.

I could write several pages about the joys of tidying up, but that's a bit beyond the scope of this book. I can, however, point you to some key resources to get you started. First, of course, is Marie Kondo's book and Netflix show. She offers a world of practical,

15 Alexis C. Madrigal, "When Did TV Watching Peak?" *The Atlantic*, May 30, 2018, https://www.theatlantic.com/technology/archive/2018/05/when-did-tv-watching-peak/561464/.

easy-to-do tips and tricks for decluttering your life. Second, you might check out *Everything That Remains* (or any other book) by Joshua Fields Millburn and Ryan Nicodemus, known online through their popular blog as The Minimalists (www.theminimalists.com). Millburn and Nicodemus focus more on the mental and emotional benefits of decluttering, so if you aren't yet convinced *why* you should trim back on all the stuff in your life, you might want to start with them.

HABITUALIZE EVERYTHING

A habit is driven by repetition and creates neural pathways in your brain that, when reinforced often enough, operate effortlessly when triggered by a stimulus. After a habit is established, it takes very little thought and energy to repeat it on a regular basis. Habits are triggered by a stimulus (time, place, reminder, alarm, and so forth), which starts a routine, which is followed by some type of reward (e.g., a pleasurable dopamine rush in your brain or some other internal or external result). A 2013 research study showed that strong habits create less of a drain on willpower and can be relied on during times of stress and low self-control.[16] In other words, habits enable you to operate on autopilot without requiring any willpower output. That means you can get things done without even touching your willpower reserves. You should therefore look to turn everything you possibly can into a habit.

To help you get started, I will list five parts of your life that can be made into habits that require little or no thought:

1. Your workout schedule should be set in stone and not debated on a daily basis. It should be a habit.
2. Your morning prayer or meditation time should be a habit. My reflection time is triggered twice a day: when I sit down at my desk at work and when I go to bed.

---

16 D.T. Neal, W. Wood, and A. Drolet, "How Do People Adhere to Goals When Will-power is Low? The Profits (and Pitfalls) of Strong Habits," *Journal of Personality and Social Psychology,* 104(6), 959.

3. Making your list of tasks for the day should be a habit, triggered either in the evening—as part of a routine of preparing for the next day—or in the morning. I create my daily task lists during my morning routine, which is triggered when I reach my desk at work.

4. How you handle the home chores that you haven't subcontracted should be a habit. For example, laundry, cleaning, and food preparation could happen regularly on Sunday afternoons.

5. Finally, anything you are doing on a repeated basis that supports your goal should be made into a habit. You will have to analyze your situation to identify these activities.

The bottom line is that habits minimize the expenditure of energy and will-power and allow for a deeper reservoir of perseverance when bigger challenges must be faced.

THE VALUE OF PERSEVERANCE

Perseverance is a key differentiator between success and failure. This chapter has condensed a lot of information into a few pages. If you have not yet begun your life-change process but are reading *Discipline Strategy* in advance of that effort, you have time to make some significant life changes that will serve you well. If you are in the middle of the process, use the quick fixes discussed in this chapter to boost your perseverance and will-power. Either way, I cannot emphasize enough the value of perseverance. Give this chapter careful consideration and do not be too quick to brush off the suggestions for change.

——————— TAKE IT FURTHER ———————

There was a lot of "meat" in this chapter, but every bit of it was designed to boost your perseverance and fuel you to reach your big goal. Put what you learned in this chapter to work for you by accessing and completing the resources listed below. You can find them for free at www.DISCIPLINESTRATEGY.com.

Obstacles and Perseverance Worksheet

As mentioned earlier in this chapter, the Obstacles and Perseverance Worksheet is designed to help you quantify the obstacle or significant challenge you're facing and prepare a plan to persevere until you solve the issue or come up with a suitable workaround. The worksheet is specifically designed to help you improve your psychological capital (PsyCap).

MyPersonality Assessment

Hopefully you've already taken the MyPersonality Assessment mentioned earlier in this book. If you haven't, do it right now! This psychometric tool will open your eyes to your innate strengths and weaknesses as they pertain specifically to the DISCIPLINE STRATEGY process. Take the test today for free at www.DISCIPLINESTRATEGY.com using the code **85285**.

PHASE

3

PERFECT AND INTENSIFY YOUR EFFORTS

CHAPTER 7

LOOP

"It's very important to have a feedback loop, where
you're constantly thinking about what you've
done and how you could be doing it better."
—ELON MUSK

A logical evaluation of how you are doing and an effective feed-back loop are necessary to fine-tune the processes and habits that are moving you toward your goal. Having just devoted a chapter to the power of perseverance and never giving up, I want to be absolutely clear that perseverance does *not* mean being blind to the need to tweak your plan, change your tactics, and strive for continuous process improvement. The ability to work the plan *until it needs to change* is necessary for success. In this chapter, we will focus on how to know when to make a change and what type of feedback loop works best.

Elon Musk, the founder of both Tesla, Inc. and SpaceX, was asked in 2017 about his biggest challenge. He replied, "One of the biggest challenges, I think, is making sure you have a corrective feedback loop, and then maintaining that corrective feedback loop over time even when people want to tell you exactly what you want to hear."[17] I first learned about feedback loops as an engineer. Engineers understand that, to use a feedback loop effectively, one must find the right data to monitor, feed them back at the right frequency, and know how to interpret and respond to the data.

My experience many years ago as a mainframe computer programmer provided another interesting perspective on feedback loops. In that environment, the feedback often came in the form of cryptic messages like "Crash dump" or "Error in module. Calculate results." Unfortunately, I had to sort through thousands of lines of code to find the problem. The feedback wasn't very helpful.

Life is often like that: the feedback is often too generic to be helpful. Thus it is critical to design your feedback loop to be specific and to include varied sources so you can make the needed revisions to your plan. Remember, this isn't about self-criticism or invoking doubt; the feedback should be constructed so that it is logical, informative, and relevant to your success.

THE GROUND-LEVEL VIEW
(WHAT THIS LOOKS LIKE IN REAL LIFE)

Elizabeth had worked hard for months to prepare for her first solo art exhibit. It would be held at a small but popular art gallery just south of the Nelson-Atkins Museum of Art in Kansas City, Missouri. Elizabeth had grown up visiting the museum with her mother at least twice a year, and she had known she wanted to be an artist since age ten. The journey to this point had been challenging. She attended the University of Missouri–Kansas City and studied studio art. The school sat just south of the Nelson-Atkins

---

17 Space Insider, "World Government Summit 2017 A Conversation with Elon Musk," YouTube video, 37:32 (cited material starting at 33:35), June 25, 2017, https://www.youtube.com/watch?v=Xa8m3SATR1s.

Museum and was a stone's throw from the site of her first private art showing.

Elizabeth had worked at a local restaurant since her college days and was now the assistant manager. She hoped this show would be a turning point that would allow her to sell enough art to quit her job. During the past year, it had seemed as if she was spending every free minute painting, perfecting new techniques, and creating sufficient inventory for her show. But she had done this work in isolation without receiving feedback from former art teachers, family, or fellow artists. As a result, she wasn't prepared for the onslaught of feedback she was about to receive.

As opening night approached, Elizabeth wondered whether she should have been more open to the direction and advice of others who had traveled this path before her. The first night went well. Many of her friends, former fellow art students, and art enthusiasts from around Kansas City showed up. But by the time the show ended three days later, the local reviews and comments on social media had identified a common criticism of her work. She realized that by operating in isolation for the past year, she had denied herself the significant value that critical feedback could have provided.

As she packed up her show, Elizabeth vowed to include some feedback from the people she trusted most before she sought another venue. But how?

THE CHALLENGES AND SOLUTIONS

Frank Sinatra's iconic song "My Way" summarizes how many of us feel about pursuing our goals. We want to do it *our own way*, in a manner that is a unique expression of ourselves. Unfortunately, this isn't always the best way to do things. I have certainly been guilty of that mindset, and it has gotten in the way of my success at times.

There are many challenges involved in logically assessing your progress and then looping back through the steps of the

DISCIPLINE STRATEGY to make adjustments. As we have all experienced, finding someone to tell you what you're doing wrong is easy, but finding the *right* person who can provide constructive, insightful, and actionable feedback is much harder. And, once you have received valuable feedback, acting on it is even more difficult.

You also need to assess yourself. Too often, we take the Snow White approach to self-assessment, looking only to pat ourselves on the back for everything we're doing well. We say, "Mirror, mirror, on the wall, who's the fairest of them all?" and then buy into our own hype. Even though it can (and will) bruise your ego, self-assessment in this context must be critical in nature and not simply highlight your successes. If you can't face your shortcomings, you'll never hit your big goals.

To clarify how and why to create a feedback loop that really works, let's examine the five big challenges most people face regarding feedback:

- **WRONG MOTIVATION:** Understanding why you want feedback and what purpose it will serve is the first critical step in the loop process. Your motivation must be to achieve clarity about your performance; feedback is not about stroking your ego.

- **NOT ASKING THE RIGHT PEOPLE:** If your Aunt Martha thought it was a mistake for you to give up that excellent job at the factory to pursue your dream of being a travel blogger, she probably won't be the best source of valued feedback. We've got to be careful who we ask for feedback and make sure we're allowing the right voices to speak into our lives.

- **FRIENDLY FIRE:** When a military force accidentally fires on its own troops, they call it a *friendly fire* incident. Asking someone you know for feedback literally *invites* friendly fire, so you must have thick skin and a process for separating quality feedback from biased opinions.

- **CRITICAL SELF-ASSESSMENT:** We all have blind spots; that's exactly why we need feedback from others in the first place. That said, no one knows you, your motivations and your struggles better than you do. Therefore, it's critical for you to be able to step back and make your own logical assessment of where you can improve.

- **FAILURE TO ACT ON FEEDBACK:** Feedback can feel like an avalanche of information. Somehow, you must decide what information is worth acting on—and what isn't. You probably can't do everything you and your advisors suggest, and it's tempting to gravitate toward the changes that seem easiest or the ones that fit your own biases. Careful prioritization, then, will be essential.

Now that we've identified the five biggest challenges in gathering feedback, let's break them down a bit more and examine how to overcome them.

CHALLENGE: WRONG MOTIVATION AND PURPOSE

It takes humility to ask for and process feedback. Your motivation should be to identify opportunities for improvement while also noting what is going well. Too many people, however, *only* want to hear about what's going well. They use positive feedback to justify what they've done and how they've done it, and they discount any negative feedback as biased or outright threatening. They allow their own biases and, if we're being honest, their egos to filter out quality feedback simply because they don't like what they're hearing. This creates a gaping blind spot in our DISCIPLINE STRATEGY process, and it's one we've got to overcome.

Positive feedback shouldn't *feed* your ego, and negative feedback shouldn't *bruise* your ego. Feedback has one purpose: to help you improve your habits and processes. It should not produce any emotional response other than increased determination. Even the most critical feedback has a purpose and can work for your good. No matter how painful it may seem at times, you should emerge from the loop feedback process with a revised and improved plan that should also increase your intrinsic motivation.

THE SOLUTION: A STRUCTURED APPROACH TO POSITIVE AND NEGATIVE FEEDBACK

Do not go into the feedback process looking to have your ego stroked. Sure, you will probably receive some positive feedback that confirms what you are doing effectively and reinforces those habits. You should certainly not overlook the value of this positive confirmation feedback. However, you need to view critical feedback—the type that shows you opportunities to improve—as equally important. Critical feedback identifies the gaps between *where you are* and *where you should be*. This is the motivation for the loop step—to identify growth and improvement opportunities.

The DISCIPLINE STRATEGY Feedback Form will guide you through a conversation designed to extract the most valuable information from someone who is offering you feedback. While you can get useful input by simply emailing this worksheet to someone and asking him or her to complete it on their own, the best and most valuable feedback will come through conversation. Download the worksheet at www.DISCIPLINESTRATEGY. com and refer to it as I explain how to use the form for maximum results. Or, if you chose not to use the form, you can use the guidelines below to lead a productive conversation designed to generate useful, actionable feedback on your progress.

First, you must clearly state your goal. This should be a brief statement that communicates your goal to the person from whom you are requesting feedback.

Second, lead the respondent through a few key questions with specific follow-up questions. You should ask:

1. **"What am I doing right?"** This question clearly solicits positive feedback. You may get confirmation of habits, effort, or self-discipline that is serving you well, but you may also gain new insights into areas of strength. Follow up by asking:
   - **"Can I intensify the things I'm doing right? If so, how?"** This question anticipates the next step in the DISCIPLINE

STRATEGY process, Intensify, which we'll discuss in the following chapter.

2. **"What am I missing?"** This open-ended question forces respondents to compare your current effort to what they would *expect* someone in your position or with your goal to do. This is why it is so important to state your goal clearly at the start of the conversation. Don't be surprised if your instinctive response to the feedback you receive is to reject what you are hearing. Listen to what they say and follow up by asking:

   - **"Why do you think this is important?"** This helps you understand and consider with an open mind whether you're actually missing something and gives you the chance to benefit from their experience, wisdom, and perspective.
   - **"How can I incorporate new habits or activities that respond to your concern?"** Here, you're looking for specific information that would support an action plan in response to the issues raised.

   At this point, keep in mind that you are in a data-gathering stage and should remain open to all ideas and suggestions. You'll sort through this information later and determine what changes should be incorporated into your plan.

3. **"What do I need to stop doing?"** This asks your respondent to identify behaviors or activities that are not supporting (and may even be harming) your goal pursuit. Expect your defenses to go up when they answer, so follow up by asking:

   - **"When have you observed me doing this?"** This asks for specific examples of this behavior. Listen carefully, take notes, and don't argue with the person. You'll likely be surprised (and perhaps a little embarrassed) by what others have noticed. It may hurt, but you need this feedback.
   - **"How can I stop these behaviors, or what can I replace them with?"** You'll likely get a variety of answers here—not all

of them useful. Listen gratefully and honestly evaluate whether the respondent's comments are worth acting on. The best case is that you'll be talking to someone who's already overcome the deficiencies they see in you and you can learn from their mistakes.

Third, close the feedback session with an open-ended question designed to extract the random thoughts that enter people's minds but that may not be expressed during a conversation. To get through to this potential gold mine, say this verbatim: **"I want you to feel comfortable in providing feedback. What else do you think I need to understand or focus on?"** Note that the question is carefully structured to give the respondent permission to speak candidly. You will often receive deeper, more philosophical reflections in response to this final question. This can leave you with fewer tactical suggestions to act on, but the comments generated may contain real gems of insight and wisdom. Follow up as appropriate, looking for more detail and understanding without disagreeing or arguing.

Again, you can certainly have this conversation freestyle, but I strongly encourage you to download the Feedback Form worksheet at www.DISCIPLINESTRATEGY.com and use it for your feedback conversations. That way, you'll have a standard, consistent system for recording feedback that makes filing, application, and later reference quick and simple.

CHALLENGE: NOT ASKING THE RIGHT PEOPLE

We all know people who are too eager to give us their feedback—whether we want to hear it or not. You most likely already know what these people think, so there is no need to ask them for a special feedback session. On the other hand, many people won't give you their feedback unless you ask for it. These people are often the ones with the most insightful and helpful information. If we simply turn to the people who are most vocal or most willing to share their opinions, we risk wasting time on those who have little additional information to offer while missing feedback from others who, though potentially difficult to reach, can provide high-value feedback.

THE SOLUTION: SEEK FEEDBACK STRATEGICALLY

For this reason, you need to identify and approach the people who can best help you assess your progress. This requires some boldness and openness. First, return to the people you consulted during the investigation phase of the DISCIPLINE STRATEGY (chapter 2). Early on, you identified them as possessing life experience and knowledge related to what you wanted to do. Second, as you've worked toward your goal, you've inevitably met new mentors and teachers or who are further along on a similar journey. Ask these people if they would be willing to give you some feedback on the major life goal you are pursuing. Use the DISCIPLINE STRATEGY Feedback Form to structure the conversation. Here's how to get started:

STEP 1: BRAINSTORM A LIST

Create an unfiltered list of people who could provide valuable feedback. Don't hesitate to write down anyone who comes to mind. There is no reason to be bashful, and you shouldn't assume people will be unwilling to help you or reluctant to provide feedback. My experience has been just the opposite: people are typically honored that you value their opinion and are eager to help.

STEP 2: REACH OUT

Once you have your list, decide how best to approach each person. Preferred communication styles vary by generation and personality. Some like to receive a phone call, while others prefer an email or text message. Keep a log of people you intend to contact, preferred contact method, contact information, and scheduled meeting times.

STEP 3: RESPECT THEIR TIME AND ATTENTION

Make it easy for people to provide feedback. Meet at a time and location that is convenient for them. Show up on time and be prepared for the discussion. If they would rather have a phone conversation, provide a copy of the Feedback Form worksheet in advance as a reference to help them organize their thoughts. Finally, if they want to respond via email, send them a copy of the worksheet, asking them to use it as a reference but to respond via email in whatever form they prefer.

STEP 4: THANK THEM

Buy some generic thank-you notes and handwrite a sincere expression of gratitude to each person who gives you feedback. Part of your advancement toward your goal is the quality of character you are developing along the way. No matter what your goal is, expressing gratitude readily and effectively should be part of your growth process. Send the thank-you note in timely fashion.

CHALLENGE: FRIENDLY FIRE

Some of the people you speak with will feel that they know what is best for you. This isn't always a bad thing, but, if they are closed-minded and emotionally charged, their feedback can turn into a self-righteous scolding. As a result, their advice may come across as needlessly harsh or negative. This is what I call *friendly fire*. In such a situation, you feel like you're being attacked—because you are!

It is important to recognize this type of response is usually driven by fear. The person has his or her own problems and is projecting them onto your situation. You could attempt to psychoanalyze the person, but what's the point? Instead, try to redirect the person's comments using the Feedback Form. That way, you can hopefully still salvage the discussion and extract whatever valuable feedback he or she may have.

SOLUTION: DEFLECT AND REDIRECT

When a friendly fire incident occurs in the military, the response consists of three steps: stop it, redirect to an appropriate target, and make sure the mistake never happens again. We will follow those general principles to deal with any instances of friendly fire you encounter while receiving feedback.

So let's break down an appropriate, time-tested response to these feedback misfires. Imagine you're soliciting feedback from your friend John on your progress toward your goal. Early in the discussion, though, John interrupts you and attempts to pick apart your overall ambitions. He goes so far as to try to convince you that your goal is not worth pursuing. Here's how you can apply the three-step response to this friendly fire situation:

1. **STOP IT:** Using the Feedback Form and discussion guide provided in this chapter should minimize the opportunity for friendly fire, but if it does occur, you need to stop it as soon as possible. You should immediately interrupt the person with something like, "John, I am surprised to hear you say that. I made the decision long ago to pursue this goal, and I'm speaking with you to get a broader perspective on how I am doing and what things I might do better. I'm not here to debate my decision. Can we continue this conversation along the lines of what I can improve or by noting what is going right? If not, then we should end the conversation now." Of course, you should use your own words, but be firm in communicating that you are intensely focused on accomplishing a specific goal and that nothing will stop you from achieving it.

2. **REDIRECT:** Once you have stopped the attack, move quickly to redirect the conversation. "John, I believe there may be an opportunity for me to improve _____. I wanted to speak with you today because I respect how you have done _____. What positive things can I learn from your experience and success in this area?" The goal is to relate an area of struggle in your situation to a success or experience

John has had. If you do this effectively, you can quickly shift the conversation to a positive tone as your respondent begins to focus on his or her own successes rather than on your alleged shortcomings.

3. **NEVER AGAIN:** Once you have encountered and managed a friendly fire incident, you'll never want to experience it again. This person, unless he or she has learned from your redirection, has shown his or her biases and is not likely to provide valuable feedback in the future. Don't seek that person's feedback going forward.

Friendly fire is not simply negative feedback or a critique; it is stumbling into an all-out assault designed to cause damage. You will know it when you see it—or, more accurately, when you *feel* it. Head it off as soon as you recognize it and take whatever steps necessary to cut that line of attack off for good.

CHALLENGE: CRITICAL SELF-ASSESSMENT

Success often requires mentors and advisors, but you can never meet everyone's expectations, and you may find that some of the advice you receive conflicts with other advice. How do you navigate around conflicting advice? One way is by using a GPS analogy. The GPS (global positioning system) in your car or on your phone operates on a geometric concept called *trilateration*. Simply put, this refers to using multiple signals from different satellites to determine your location. Similarly, when you go through the feedback process, you are receiving multiple signals from different vantage points, and each signal gives you some insight into where you are and how you're doing. While each signal is important, you want to pay special attention to where the signals overlap or complement each other. In a moment, I'll show you when and how to compare this overlapping feedback to your own thoughts on your progress. Agreement between these external signals and your personal self-assessment will lock in your location and show you exactly where you are on your path to the goal.

SOLUTION: TAKE AN HONEST LOOK AT YOURSELF

All this external, third-party feedback—especially the overlapping feedback—helps you improve your *self*-assessment by shining light on areas that you may have overlooked. Armed with quality insights from people you trust, you're ready to complete a self-assessment using the DISCIPLINE STRATEGY Self-Assessment and Action Plan worksheet. You can download a copy at www. DISCIPLINESTRATEGY.com and use it to get a handle on how well *you* think you're doing. Your self-assessment should be an honest account of where you are struggling to improve your performance. You want to identify the gaps between where you are and where your goal indicates you want to be at some specific time in the future.

In chapter 4, you conceived a plan that was specific to your unique goal and life situation. This plan identified a gap between where you started and where you will finish. That gap should be closing as a result of plan implementation and perseverance through difficulties. However, the loop process forces you to get external feedback that then informs your own self-assessment. You should, therefore, think of your self-assessment as a mini-plan within your broader plan. It is a tweak of, or perhaps even a major repair to, the plan.

SELF-ASSESSMENT (SWOT) AND
ACTION PLAN WORKSHEETS

The Self-Assessment (SWOT) and Action Plan worksheets are designed to guide you through the self-assessment process and help you incorporate the external feedback you've received. Print the forms now and follow along with the following explanation. Again, if you chose not to use the provided worksheets, you can still perform a similar self-assessment using this process.

Using the Self-Assessment (SWOT) Worksheet, I want you to
focus on your perception of your strengths, weaknesses, opportunities and threats. It is a common business tool for strategic planning, and it also works well in assessing your progress toward
your goal. First, what are you doing right? Where are you on
course or even ahead of your plan? Don't limit your comments
to the feedback you've received; think for yourself and see if your
respondents missed anything you think is noteworthy. Also, identify which of these strengths were observed by one or more feedback sources. If you agree with the strength identified and have
one or more external confirmations, consider the observation
accurate—the GPS is working! Finally, look for ways to leverage
this strength in other areas.

Second, focus on your weaknesses or the (sometimes
surprising) areas where you think you're falling short. Again, look
back at your original goal and where you thought you'd be by
now. If you've missed a milestone or haven't achieved measurable results yet, try to understand why. Sometimes, these missteps
point to an internal struggle you haven't faced yet, such as
emotional difficulties, health/fatigue issues, frustration, or lack of
enjoyment. These are issues only you can identify; your feedback
respondents probably didn't mention much about your emotional
health!

The external feedback may have unearthed other weaknesses than what you saw in your self-assessment. Consider these
comments carefully because our natural tendency is to quickly
reject this type of feedback. And again, as with strengths, highlight any weakness that was confirmed by both your self-assessment and one or more external feedback sources. Finally, consider
potential solutions or actions that would help to eliminate each
weakness.

The third item in the SWOT analysis is *opportunities*. An opportunity may be something that has newly emerged through your
experience as you work toward your goal, or it may simply be
something you missed at the start. Opportunities may also manifest

themselves in response to strengths or weaknesses. Once you're experienced in thinking about your strengths and weaknesses, opportunities may begin to manifest themselves long before you complete this self-assessment. Because you have trained you reticular activating system to be constantly aware of your goal and to search for supporting information, you should already have a mental list of opportunities. Combine these with the ones your feedback sources identified, always looking for multiple confirmations to identify the strongest candidates. Brainstorm ways to pursue and benefit from these opportunities.

That brings us to the fourth SWOT area, *threats*. Understanding threats is critical. You need to define and dissect them and perhaps even seek additional advice on potential solutions from an outside source. A threat is something that could totally destroy or severely damage the chances of reaching your goal. As such, it is much more serious than a weakness.

A threat can be internal or external. An internal threat might be an action, thought, habit, or a poor decision you have made. An external threat is something you can't control or prevent and that may require action on your part to avoid. Before you can leverage your insights regarding your strengths, weaknesses, and opportunities, you must first deal directly and firmly with threats.

The last part of your self-assessment is reviewing your progress toward the stepping stones established in your original plan. These can easily be forgotten or ignored, so don't make that mistake. Fully assess how you've performed relative to your stepping stones. Did you fall short? Were you ahead of schedule? What can you learn from your performance at these critical points?

If you're using the forms provided online, now pull out the Action Plan Worksheet. This worksheet walks you through a process to help you plan a response to your Self-Assessment (SWOT) Analysis. Begin by transferring your refined strengths, weaknesses, opportunities, and threats to the Action Plan. Clearly state each one, what action you'll take as a result of this new understanding, and some ideas for how you'll continually monitor and reassess each area. I also encourage you to name an accountability partner whom you've given permission to check in on these things.

Taking such a close, honest look at ourselves can be difficult— far more difficult than accepting the feedback of other people. However, we'll never reach the big goals we've set for ourselves if we don't stop to perform regular self-checkups. External sources can give us a wealth of information, but those data points can't help us get a fix on our current position if we fail to consider the most critical signal: ourselves.

CHALLENGE: FAILURE TO ACT ON FEEDBACK

The final step in this chapter is to loop the feedback and self-assessment back into the DISCIPLINE STRATEGY process to make any needed changes. You may revise the plan conceived in chapter 4 or just make some adjustments in implementation. In any case, this loop step must result in a list of actions designed to guide your improvement, whether minor or significant, of your original plan.

SOLUTION: REVISE THE ORIGINAL PLAN

If you have found reasons to make significant evidence-based changes, you may choose to revise your original plan document. Even if you have to make huge changes, keep in mind this is not at all uncommon and should not be perceived as a failure. It is extremely difficult to develop a perfect plan, and there is no better teacher than experience.

So if you realize plan revisions are called for, you should take all you've learned from the feedback and self-assessment and go back to the investigation stage of the DISCIPLINE STRATEGY. Don't rush into this, though. Be sure the changes are truly legitimate and wise and that you're not simply overreacting to your new understanding of your situation. Take time to absorb the new information you've obtained and investigate the relevant issues. Then, if necessary, revise your plan based on the solid research and knowledge that have come from your experience, feedback, and self-assessment.

DON'T OVERDO IT

Although some situations may require you to go back to the drawing board and completely rework your original plan, it is usually sufficient to compose a *supplemental* action plan that focuses your energies and habit-formation efforts in the few areas that need the most attention. As you get new information and feedback throughout your plan implementation, loop those new insights back into the process and see where or if any tweaks are needed. If so, run back through the SWOT analysis and update the Action Plan form. Everything you've done in this loop step— receiving feedback from multiple sources and completing a self-assessment—should have generated a lot of ideas on how best to address the identified strengths, weaknesses, opportunities, and threats, so put all that great information to work for you!

——— TAKE IT FURTHER ———

This chapter had detailed explanations of three different worksheets, all of which you can download for free at www. DISCIPLINESTRATEGY.com. As a reminder, this chapter's three worksheets are:

Feedback Form

Asking friends and colleagues for honest feedback can be a tricky proposition. Without clear guidelines, well-meaning respondents could simply tell us what they think we want to hear, give us a broad overview with no specifics, or even try to talk us out of our goals. Avoid these common feedback pitfalls by walking your feedback source through a clear, actionable conversation using the questions and categories on this form.

Self-Assessment (SWOT) Worksheet

We are too often our own worst critics. We generally think either too highly of ourselves or we only see our failures; neither option provides valuable insights. The Self-Assessment Worksheet, however, guides you in an honest look at yourself and equips you to list your strengths, weaknesses, opportunities, and threats in an effective, unbiased way.

Action Plan Worksheet

Taking the results of the Self-Assessment (SWOT) Worksheet, the Action Plan Worksheet walks you through the development of a plan to magnify strengths, minimize weaknesses, exploit opportunities, and eliminate threats.

CHAPTER 8

INTENSIFY

*"Always work hard. Intensity clarifies. It creates
not only momentum but also the pressure you
need to feel either friction or fulfillment."*
—Marcus Buckingham

Whatever journey you are on, there comes a time when you must intensify your efforts to cross over into your new life. This season of intensity can make a significant difference. When you launch a rocket, for example, you have to accelerate to an escape velocity in order to leave Earth's gravitational pull. Most of the rocket's fuel actually burns up during the launch; getting it off the ground is the hardest part of the journey. Similarly, in your change effort, you have to push hard to ingrain your new habits, reach the payoff of years of effort, and safely escape the past as you create momentum toward the future. I call this step the *intensity push*.

I use the term *season of intensity* because you can expect a period of internal doubt and external criticism when you commit at the level I suggest. Recognizing that this is just a season and not a permanent experience is important both for your own equilibrium and for explaining to others what you are doing. Living an unbalanced life that is almost entirely focused on your goal is not sustainable over the long term, but it is a necessary component of your success in the short term. Put simply, your whole world will need to revolve around your goal for a brief season if you want to achieve an effective liftoff.

This step comes naturally after you have gotten well into implementation and have had a chance to make a logical feedback loop to improve what you are doing. Trying to intensify your efforts while you are still learning can temporarily lead you off track, however. The time to intensify is after you've gained sufficient experience to know you're pointed in the right direction.

In his 2012 *Harvard Business Review* article, "How Hard Are You Willing to Push Yourself?" Tony Schwartz noted:

What do all people who achieve true excellence and consistently high performance have in common? The answer isn't great genes, although they're nice to have. It's the willingness to push themselves beyond their current limits day in and day out, despite the discomfort that creates, the sacrifice of more immediate gratification, and the uncertainty they'll be rewarded for their efforts.[18]

Intensity is just that—the willingness to push yourself beyond what you think you're capable of; it's the rocket fuel that pushes you over the finish line!

---

18 Tony Schwartz, "How Hard Are You Willing to Push Yourself?" *Harvard Business Review*, July 2, 2012, https://hbr.org/2012/07/how-hard-are-you-willing-to-pu.html.

THE GROUND-LEVEL VIEW
(WHAT THIS LOOKS LIKE IN REAL LIFE)

Jack made a few missteps during his first attempt at college. After graduating from a rural high school in Alabama, he headed west to attend the University of Denver—his dream since age fourteen. The dream was so compelling that Jack actually focused harder in his classes, stepped up his efforts on the soccer team, and even convinced his parents to pay for an SAT tutor. Before his senior year started, Jack had already been offered a full scholarship to play soccer at the University of Denver. It appeared that his dream would come true.

Surprisingly, though, by the end of his first semester of college, Jack was struggling. He found being away from the familiar environment of his small hometown was much more difficult than he expected. His roommate, though a nice guy, was loud, frequently high, and awake at odd hours of the day. The rigors of a high-level college soccer program also left Jack little energy or time to study. At the end of the first semester, Jack was on academic probation. By the end of the first year, despite the diligent efforts of the athletic department and counseling office to keep him academically eligible, Jack found himself back home and out of college with no idea how he would recover from this stunning setback.

Jack's employment opportunities were limited in his hometown. He got a night-shift job at a local manufacturing business and lived with his parents. After several months of enduring this new routine, Jack was determined to find a path to a better place. His search for new options led him to an online degree program offered by the University of West Alabama. Since living at home greatly reduced his expenses, Jack could afford the tuition costs. He started slowly, taking just two classes per semester, and he began to integrate study time into his life. Without the distractions he had encountered at the University of Denver, Jack excelled. His high motivation for a life change boosted his ability to focus and persevere.

After two years of part-time study (including summers) plus the credits he was able to transfer from Denver, Jack was sixty-two credit hours short of a bachelor's degree. After some detailed planning with his college counselor, Jack knew what he had to do: he would major in Engineering Technology within the College of Business and Technology, combine this education with his job experience in manufacturing, and some day start his own niche manufacturing company. He had a clear goal for his life and was performing well in his classes. He had persevered through some difficult times and received some helpful feedback from several advisors. It was time for him to intensify his efforts.

Jack decided that he would quit his job, push himself hard through three back-to-back semesters of twenty-one credit hours each (seven classes a semester), and graduate in twelve months. For those twelve months, he would bring his intense focus to bear be on attending online and on-campus classes and studying. He was confident that he could do it—as long as he kept his eyes on the potential pitfalls of such an aggressive plan.

THE CHALLENGES AND SOLUTIONS

Creating a period of intensity will freak some people out. First, you will make other people feel insecure if they are not as intense and focused as you are. That's their problem, not yours. Second, you will not be able to spend as much time with friends or family as they are accustomed to, so they will feel neglected. Third, people will think you're acting abnormally (because you will be). All this change will scare some people, even those who know you well. Finally, your growth and progress during this season will transform you into a new person with a new life. A new horizon is appearing. Parts of your old life and habits will fade away, and some old relationships will end. These can all be scary propositions.

Intensifying your efforts is about making difficult choices, saying no to distractions, and removing all unnecessary time expenditures from your life. If you do this right, you will have a lot of people scratching their head. If someone calls you crazy, that's probably a sign that you're on the right path! Let's address the intensify step head-on with specific strategies, anticipated problems, and solid solutions. The main challenges and problems you'll have to navigate are:

- **OVERCOMMITMENT:** To move faster and focus with intensity, you must lighten your load—i.e., remove all the things in your life that are not completely necessary. We will discuss how to identify these and how you can remove them from your life as diplomatically as possible, even if only temporarily.

- **CLUTTERED COGNITIVE SPACE:** During your intensity push, you will not have the time and energy to think about many things outside your focus area. In addition to lightening your load in terms of time and responsibility, you will also need additional cognitive space.

- **OVERCOMING BAD HABITS:** The foundation for intensity is healthy habits. I have stressed the need for healthy habits many times. At this juncture, before you intensify, make sure you have the support systems in place that will empower this burst of intensity.

- **COGNITIVE ISSUES:** Concentrating fully is a real challenge for some people. Healthy habits solve most such issues, but some people may benefit from medications designed to improve mental clarity and focus. We will look at the options.

- **UNFOCUSED MIND:** Mind control and games will help you deal with your burst of intensity, reduce stress, and improve motivation. Controlling your mind and keeping it focused on your short-term task list through a game-based reward system can enhance the productivity of your intensity push.

- **BURNOUT:** Burnout is a risk during the intensifying phase. Several strategies, in addition to the items mentioned, can allow you to operate on the edge while avoiding burnout.

- **COMING OUT OF WARP SPEED:** In the popular *Star Trek* series, some danger was always involved when transitioning out of warp speed. You could wind up in a part of the galaxy you didn't recognize or find yourself face to face with an unexpected villain. As your period of intensity winds down, you should take some steps to avoid creating unexpected stresses.

These are eight pretty big problems, so let's break them down and identify the best solutions for blasting through, around, or over them.

CHALLENGE: OVERCOMMITMENT

How many times have you fallen into bed exhausted from a full day of activities and crying, "I'm too busy!"? It's a common complaint in our society, but the *busy syndrome* is a choice. You get to choose where and how you spend your time, and most of us choose way too many things. And no matter how much we try to dress our busyness up as productivity, the truth is most people stay busy with unimportant activities that do little—if anything—to bring them closer to reaching their goals.

Changing your typical life patterns can be painful, but pain is often a necessary component of growth and advancement. Moreover, radical change is crucial for a successful intensity push. When you hit this step in the DISCIPLINE STRATEGY process, I encourage you to strip everything out of your life that is not mission-critical. Your focus will be on maximizing your routines, work effort, and time investment to create as much momentum toward your goal as possible.

SOLUTION: TRADE BUSY FOR INTENSELY FOCUSED

In an earlier chapter, I suggested strategies for reducing the amount of time you spend on less important activities. Now, during your intensity push, I suggest you take that even further and completely stop doing *everything* except the specific tasks that propel you toward your goal. I want you to work harder than you have ever worked before. You may still be clinging to the notion that you simply don't have time to put any more effort into your goal. It's my job to show you that you're wrong. There's always a little more effort to give and a little more time to reclaim. If you need some direction, consider the following temporary sacrifices.

First, you should stop watching all TV for a little while. Most people have a habit of shutting down in the evening and flipping on the television or computer for some relaxation. They act like the same button that turns the TV *on* also turns their brains *off*. During your intensity push, work past this artificial cutoff time that you've created for yourself. The best way to handle TV and computer distractions is to go cold turkey. Don't even turn it on in the evenings. Instead, work toward your goal. If you are a student, study longer. If you are an entrepreneur, extend the time spent working on specific high-value business activities. If you are training for an Ironman, go to bed earlier or invest additional time in areas where you are weak. Your evening routine typically contains low-hanging fruit for cutting out waste. Do it.

Second, subcontract everything you can, be it mowing the yard, getting groceries, fixing the ceiling fan, or painting the house. In today's "gig economy," where app-based technologies have greatly simplified how you can engage short-term help, there is no reason not to get rid of tasks that don't support your goal pursuit. Before committing to any task, ask yourself, *Do I have to do this, or can I hire someone to do it for me?* If someone else *can*, let them. Check out services like TaskRabbit.com and see what kind of help is available in your area.

Third, set a high bar for other activities. I've come to evaluate these opportunities on the *Heck yes!* (HY) scale. I learned this from my company's hiring practices; it took me a few years to realize that the only people I should hire were the ones who elicited a "Heck yes" from everyone who interviewed or interacted with the job candidate. This same criterion should be applied to any invitations that are outside your goal focus.

Base your HY ratings on *importance*, not fun. Should you attend your grandmother's one-hundredth birthday? Heck yes! Should you attend the reunion concert for Guns N' Roses next weekend? As enjoyable as that might be, the clear answer is *no*. This isn't complicated. During your intensity push, some things in life are important and some are not. Your goal and your life-change process are at the top of your agenda. You are in a phase of intensity to make sure you reach this goal. In this situation, there shouldn't be many events outside your goal pursuit that get a strong HY rating.

Fourth, change your self-talk. Stop telling everyone, including yourself, how busy you are. Instead, change your self-talk and the way you speak to others. Rather than saying, "I'm too busy!" speak the truth of the situation. You might say, "I am very focused on an important goal right now and have chosen to invest the bulk of my time in pursuit of that goal. I will not always be this intense and engaged, but it is what I've chosen for now, and I am excited about the progress I am making." You are not busy, scattered, unfocused, out of control, or confused; rather, you are focused, driven, motivated, on target, and accelerating to escape velocity. You aren't a victim to circumstances any longer. You're at the wheel and making your own informed decisions about who and what needs your time and attention during this season, so be clear in explaining the situation correctly to yourself and to others.

The most common objection I get whenever I walk people through this part of the process is, "But Tim, I'm married and have young children. Surely you aren't suggesting I neglect my family so I can focus on my goal, are you?" Of course not. Nothing is more important to me than my wife and children, and that's been true throughout my entire adult life—even back when I spent my lunch hours crammed in the backseat of my car cranking out code on a borrowed laptop. Yes, you will probably see your family a little less for a season, so be sure to get your spouse's or partner's buy-in before putting such severe restrictions on your time. But I would never suggest you outright neglect your family. Your goal will cause you to make many sacrifices; do whatever it takes to make sure your family isn't one of them.

CHALLENGE: CLUTTERED COGNITIVE SPACE

As wasteful as non-productive activities are, the even tougher gremlin to fight during your time of intensity is your cognitive space. If you allow it, your mind will always be filled with different questions and scenarios that do nothing to support your plan implementation or goal pursuit. This jumbled mix of useless thoughts is what's called *cognitive load*. Technically, cognitive load refers to the burden you are putting on your working memory in any given moment. You can think of it like a batch of background computer processes, always churning away in the back of your mind and taking up a piece of your precious mental capacity.

For example, say your friend John invited you to the Guns N' Roses concert mentioned previously, but you said no as part of your short-term, absolute focus on your goal. You could waste time thinking, *Why did John act so mad when I told him I couldn't go to the concert with him? I hope he doesn't think I never want to hang out with him.* Ruminating on questions you can never answer is a drain you don't need. Worrying about anything that has no solution, serves no purpose, and does not support your goal is a waste of mental capacity. Your mind simply will not be productive if it is constantly distracted by worry, obsessive thoughts, or doubt. You must give yourself permission to free up cognitive space, allowing efficient use of the mental energy required during this time.

SOLUTION: NOTE AND REMOVE DISTRACTIONS

I want to recommend two strategies for reducing cognitive load. First, I suggest you create a *mystery bucket*. This may sound silly, but it really is what the name implies: a place to drop (and then forget) the questions you can never answer that may otherwise get stuck in your mind. Your mystery box can be imaginary or real, such as a little box you can drop notes into. I prefer to use an imaginary mystery bucket and simply visualize putting something into it. If I were in the Guns N' Roses concert situation, I might simply say, "John reacted badly when I said I couldn't go to the concert. I hate that, but there's nothing else I can do about it. So, I'm going to drop that experience in my mystery bucket and move on."

I should be clear that this works only with things you don't *have* to understand or address in order to reach your goal. More specifically, if your plan requires you to wake up at 5:00 a.m. every morning to complete something (studying, writing, swimming, or getting to work), your inability to get out of bed at 5:00 a.m. cannot be assigned to the mystery bucket. You actually have to figure that one out. However, if you are displeased with some political development or social phenomenon, stow it in the mystery bucket immediately. If it helps to keep a small container under your desk or beside your trash can labeled *Mystery Bucket*, then do so. You can write the items you are assigning to the mystery bucket on small pieces of paper and toss them into the bucket. Once something has been assigned to the mystery bucket, you no longer think about it.

Second, you should create some kind of file tickler system. In chapter 5, I briefly mentioned the tickler system I use to process emails. This is a great way to efficiently manage email-based information. However, it is also a great way to prioritize tasks and remove the sense of urgency sometimes associated with things that just don't matter. If you get an email that is not related to the pursuit of your goal but you feel it stealing some brain power in the moment, assign it to a future day for further consideration.

For example, suppose you receive an email on January 5 about an upcoming convention in May. You immediately begin debating whether you should go. Instead of letting something like this distract you from your goal pursuit, immediately place the email into your tickler folder called "March." Now, you can forget about the item for two months. You will process all March emails on March 1. By then, you will be more capable of making an informed decision about whether to go to that convention. Besides, items placed in the tickler file often don't seem very important when they come back up for consideration.

CHALLENGE: OVERCOMING BAD HABITS

I have stressed the need for healthy habits throughout the DISCIPLINE STRATEGY. If you haven't sensed their importance up to now, you will almost certainly recognize it once you embark on a time of increased intensity. Up to this point, you may have been able to make progress without a focus on healthy habits and life routines, but now you'll pay a price if you don't have them established.

SOLUTION: REVIEW, EVALUATE, AND DECIDE

No matter how old you are, it's never too late to review your life habits, evaluate their appropriateness and effectiveness, and decide to go in a new direction. We don't need to rehash the specific issues we've discussed in earlier chapters, but below is a chart to bring the key points of those different discussions together.

Hopefully, you've already identified some opportunities to improve in this arena throughout the previous chapters. As a result, you may already have some action items designed to improve your habits. If so, great! If not, this is yet another opportunity for you to take action in these important areas.

CHALLENGE: COGNITIVE ISSUES

Many will argue that today's common diagnosis of ADHD (Attention Deficit/Hyperactivity Disorder) is overblown or just

Area of Life	Healthy and Efficient Habits and Lifestyle
Diet	There are several healthy diet options. Find one that works for you and stick to it. Efficiently prepare food in batches. Avoid processed and unhealthy foods. Make healthy eating a habit and a routine, not a meal-by-meal decision.
Fitness	Maintain a regular fitness program that includes resistance training, aerobic/cardiovascular exercise, and some high-intensity interval training (taking any physical limitations into account, of course). Your ability to work long hours and to persevere through difficulties will depend in part on your physical fitness.
Routines	How you do laundry, chores, and grocery shopping should all be efficient, well-thought-out routines designed to support good habits but minimize the amount of time invested. For example, if you eat the same healthy meals repetitively, buy the needed ingredients in bulk or maintain a shopping list that can be printed and not created from scratch each week. Everything in your life that you do at least once a week should be examined for potential improvements in efficiency. Yes, you will begin to look like a robot at times, but this will be a very small part of your week. The rest of the week, you will look like the beast you are!
Emotion	Emotions can support success or totally sabotage your progress. Part of fueling healthy habits is maintaining level and balanced emotions. This will occur naturally when the items described above are running smoothly. Also, meditation, mindfulness, and spiritual habits will help your emotions remain friendly. One way to support healthy emotions is to avoid negative people. Even if they are close friends or family, you don't need negativity during your intensity push. Avoid these people.

a way for pharmaceutical companies to sell more drugs. Others consider ADHD a true epidemic with widespread social and economic impact. I will not pick a side in that argument. My desire is that all of us could feel such passion and excitement for our goals that our bodies and brains produce whatever chemicals we need to help us achieve them. Unfortunately, from my firsthand observations, I don't believe that will always happen. As I've seen over and over again through my personal coaching sessions, people struggle—some more than you would think. And sometimes, no amount of healthy eating, diet, quality sleep, or positive self-talk will solve a person's cognitive struggles ... without a little help.

SOLUTION: THE WONDERS OF MODERN MEDICINE

When I was in college, I felt blessed with a brain that could focus for hours on complex math and engineering classes. When I was juggling work, learning to fly, and double-majoring in math and engineering at Vanderbilt University, I'd argue that I could focus intensely for twenty hours a day. Even as a young parent working a corporate day job and writing code into the wee hours of the morning for my startup software company, I could concentrate and do complex tasks like a machine. Ah, the joys of youth!

Then, about the time I turned forty, my physician confirmed that I had inherited my family's predisposition for early heart disease and convinced me I needed to take a statin drug to lower my cholesterol. Unfortunately, taking a statin introduced me to major brain fog. When I visited one of the nation's top cardiologists to discuss the issue, he was adamant that the statin wasn't causing the brain fog. He thought it was some type of unrelated ADHD or depression-like symptom. It took many years for my doctors and me to conclude that the statins were indeed the cause of the fog. We found other effective strategies to manage my heart disease, and the fog lifted within a couple months after I stopped taking the statin medication. However, this experience gave me firsthand knowledge of ADHD-type symptoms. I now have a high level of empathy for those who struggle with any sort of attention issue, and I recognize the potentially limiting, if not debilitating, effects of such challenges.

But—and you knew a big *but* was coming—you cannot allow ADHD to become an excuse or limiting factor in today's sophisticated medical world. It is an issue that can be resolved, just like being out of shape or overweight. If you believe ADHD or other cognitive issues are working against your goal pursuit, try these steps for getting back on track:

1. Clean up your life, diet, and routines and see if you get any relief from your ADHD. If you do these things and the ADHD limitations continue, or if you can't muster the motivation to make lifestyle changes, then proceed to Step 2.

2. If your insurance plan allows it, skip your family doctor and go straight to a psychiatrist who specializes in ADHD. You will get a detailed ADHD evaluation and have a discussion with the doctor so he or she can fully understand your challenges. The doctor will most likely suggest medication. If you agree to take the medication, then consider Step 3.

3. The pharmaceutical company's standard recommended starting dose for a medication is not necessarily the lowest *effective* dose for your biochemistry. Typically, it is the dose that provides the best benefits with the fewest side effects for the most people. What's required for the masses may not be exactly what's required for you. So, discuss with your doctor the option of starting with a very low dose and increasing slowly if needed until you find the dose that works for you. This will minimize side effects, extend the usefulness of the drug, and still yield significant benefits.

4. Do your homework before seeing the doctor and become familiar with the various possible medications. Older medications that may be used off-label for ADHD may be most effective. Doctors tend to prescribe medications that are newer, costlier, and pushed by the pharmaceutical companies. Use your research skills, as discussed in chapter 2, to find a list of ADHD drugs. Then research patients' experiences with these medications. Also, go to Google Scholar and read the abstracts of as many research studies on the drugs as you can. Finally, be prepared to discuss the following medications that are often left out of the discussion:

   - **Bupropion (Wellbutrin):** First made in 1969 but not approved for medical use in the United States until 1989, bupropion increases levels of dopamine and norepinephrine, two neurotransmitters. It is available in a variety of forms: instant release, sustained release, and extended release. Since it is available as a generic medication, it is inexpensive. Bupropion is highly effective in increasing mental focus, clarity, and energy.

- **Trazodone (many brand names):** Developed in Italy in the 1960s as a new form of antidepressant, it quickly gained a bad reputation for making people sleepy and has recently become widely used to treat insomnia. ADHD can often be aggravated by lack of sleep. Trazodone addresses this issue when taken in small doses (12.5 to 25 mg) before bedtime. It improves sleep quality and, as a result, enhances one's ability to focus during the day. Recent research published in the academic journal *Brain* touts Trazadone as a "potential new disease-modifying treatment for dementia."[19] Trazodone can often solve sleep deficits that contribute to ADHD while also protecting your brain from dementia.

- **Modafinil (Provigil):** This is the only drug approved for fatigue management by the U.S. Air Force. Astronauts on the International Space Station have also used Modafinil to combat fatigue and improve performance. The drug, invented in the 1970s and introduced as a medication in 1986, was originally designed to treat narcolepsy. The research shows low potential for addiction or abuse. Public forums that discuss individual experiences with Modafinil generally recommend starting with very low doses and titrating up until benefit is achieved. In 2004, a robust research study published in *Biological Psychiatry* stated that Modafinil can be an effective therapy for ADHD, with an effect similar to that of stimulants but without the side effects that commonly accompany the use

19 M. Halliday, H. Radford, K.A. Zents, C. Molloy, J.A. Moreno, N.C. Verity, E. Smith, C.A. Ortori, D.A. Barrett, M. Bushell, and G.R. Malluci, "Repurposed drugs targeting eIF2α-P-mediated translational repression prevent neurodegeneration in mice," *Brain*, 140(6), 1,768–1,783.

of amphetamine-like drugs.[20] You may want to take copies of research studies with you to your appointment if you want to convince your doctor to prescribe this drug.

I realize this topic is controversial, and I've condensed a lot of information into just a couple of pages. But people who are otherwise extremely capable can get fired or miss opportunities for advancement because they have failed to deal with their ADHD or other cognitive challenges. Whatever your goal is, don't let untreated cognitive issues be your downfall. Take personal ownership of the issue, read and study the body of knowledge available, try every lifestyle change you can, and then go the pharmaceutical route if necessary.

I will caution you again, however: don't blindly follow a doctor's recommendation without doing your own research. You need to be able to have an intelligent, well-informed conversation with your doctor about how you feel, what challenges you're facing, and what solutions you'd like to explore. Otherwise, you could end up with a knee-jerk prescription to a drug that may work well for the masses but misses the mark for you.

CHALLENGE: UNFOCUSED MIND

During a time of intensity, you will face both physical and mental challenges. Your brain will try at times to slow you down or even *shut* you down. You have to use various mind games to stay focused and to keep the internal naysayers at bay.

SOLUTION: PRACTICE MIND CONTROL

I went through a season when I was running one business, starting another business, and working on a Ph.D. The well-known and

20 D.C. Turner, L. Clark, J. Dowson, T.W. Robbins, and B.J. Sahakian, "Modafinil improves cognition and response inhibition in adult attention-deficit/hyperactivity disorder," *Biological Psychiatry*, 55(10), 1,031–1,040.

often-used phrase "one day at a time" became a meaningful mind-control technique for me. By *mind control*, I'm not talking about a stage show hypnotist convincing you to cluck like a chicken in front of all your friends for laughs. Mind control is the ability to focus your mental energy during a predetermined span of time for an intentional purpose.

During your intensity push, your mind will often fight you with negative thoughts or attempts at long-term forecasting that can lead to doubt and frustration. Once you have reached this point in the DISCIPLINE STRATEGY, you have already decided, debated, investigated, and put your heart and soul into the pursuit of your goal. You must now control your mind to undertake the daily grind, which includes the specific actions and daily tasks you believe will move you toward your goal. It is not time to debate, analyze, or reconsider; that is behind you. It is time to execute.

During my own intensity push, I chose to focus on one day at a time. I would start my day by reviewing what I was doing and making specific plans about what needed to be accomplished that day. If my mind tried to go anywhere other than that day's activities and task list, I controlled it by reminding myself, *One day at a time*. This became an effective and automatic response to a thought like, *How in the world am I going to read seven hundred pages for school this week and spend the necessary time with our software development team at work while also making progress on an important consulting project?* Obviously, that question has no immediate answer and only creates feelings of stress and doubt. By training my mind to always respond instantly with *one day at a time*, I could let go of the phantom question and return my focus to the day's tasks. With few exceptions, I always got through the day successfully, and everything fell into place over time.

PLAY MIND GAMES

Gamification—using game elements to encourage engagement—has become a popular adaptation from the video-gaming world. It is used for marketing promotions (McDonald's Monopoly game) and loyalty programs. There are as many different forms of gamification as there are games. It works too. A comprehensive research study in 2014, presented at the forty-seventh Hawaii International Conference on System Science, concluded that gamification increases motivation and improves results.[21]

For our purposes, a game is simply a form of play guided by rules and won through effort. What I am suggesting then is that you find a way to gamify your period of intensity. Keep it simple but fun. Establish the rules of the game, with the victory coming after you have accomplished certain tasks or reached milestones. Let the reward be enjoyable and maybe even something you've temporarily given up during your intensity push—a night out on the town or a movie with friends. Your game has to be straightforward, easy to understand and track, and with a legitimate reward at stake.

For example, perhaps you are working intensely on a dissertation. Your game rules may state that you write every evening from 5:00 p.m. to 9:00 p.m. and that you cannot touch your remote control during the week. However, if you surpass your writing goals for the day by 9:00 p.m., you can reward yourself with a half hour of your favorite TV show before bed. That gives you a clear set of rules, an easy way to know if you've *won* for the day, and a simple reward that you enjoy.

An entire industry has popped up to support gamification with apps, software, and communities. However, this can be a huge danger zone for you. Ironically, these attempts at fostering focus through gamification have resulted in a world of distractions. You could waste hours looking at the different gamification options and thinking up elaborate reward systems. You don't need that! Simply make up something simple, doable, and enjoyable that boosts your motivation.

---

21 I. Caponetto, J. Earp, and M. Ott, "Gamification and education: A literature review," *European Conference on Games Based Learning* Vol 1, Academic Conferences International Limited, 50.

CHALLENGE: BURNOUT

Burnout is not just a modern-day term people throw around when they feel frustrated or overworked. Rather, it is a solidly established concept that has been extensively researched and studied for more than forty years. It is defined as a state of physical and mental exhaustion caused by one's professional life, often following a period of high enthusiasm and effort. It can be hard to recover from burnout, so it is critical to anticipate and prevent this threat during your intensity push.

SOLUTION: KNOW YOUR LIMITS AND BUILD YOUR RESOURCES

The first signs of burnout are chronic exhaustion and a sense that some type of mental distance is hampering your efforts to reach your goal. It may manifest itself through excuses, overeating, sleeping late, avoidance, or any of a dozen other cues. Much of what I have presented in this chapter is designed to remove unnecessary workload so you can pursue your goal with intensity. But despite putting these strategies to work, you may still find yourself on the edge of the canyon called burnout.

Avoiding burnout requires understanding your personality and finding the limits of your capacity. This threshold is different for each of us. Hopefully by now, you've completed the MyPersonality Assessment at www.DISCIPLINESTRATEGY. com that is included for free with the purchase of this book. This personality test measures six personality dimensions and generates a detailed report on your personality traits and how they may impact parts of the DISCIPLINE STRATEGY process. Pay close attention to your burnout report, which will give you specific avoidance strategies based on your personality.

Another way to avoid burnout is to make sure you have sufficient resources to do what you are trying to do. If you try to pull off an intense effort without the needed resources, frustration and burnout are likely to ensue. These resources might take the form of time, people, money, cognitive ability, or other things. Although stretching your capabilities and resources is typically part of intensity, you can't create things out of thin air. Therefore, before starting your period of intensity, take stock of whether you have everything you need to get the job done. If you don't, stop and get the needed resources in place first.

CHALLENGE: COMING OUT OF WARP SPEED

Introduced in the novel *Islands of Space* and popularized by *Star Trek*, *warp speed* has become a popular term for the highest attainable speed. That's how I want you to imagine your period of intensity. For a season, you've eliminated all other distractions, put the right resources in place, fed your mind and body exactly what it needs to perform at a high level, and, as a result, you've covered more ground in less time than you ever thought possible. You're moving at warp speed! That's great, but you can't stay there forever. Once you've cruised at warp speed long enough to achieve its intended purpose, it's time to transition back to a slower speed.

SOLUTION: TRANSITION WITH INTENTION AND PREPARATION

Transitioning out of warp speed requires intention and preparation. To initiate your time of intensity, you made several life changes, some of them significant. You have established new habits and eliminated others that did not serve you well. These changes may have had a noticeably positive impact on your life.

Although you may no longer need to live at such a high level of intensity, you probably don't want to go back to where you were prior to this phase of the DISCIPLINE STRATEGY, either. Before you decelerate out of warp speed, make an intentional plan about what your new lifestyle will be and prepare accordingly. Here are some suggestions:

LET GOOD HABITS STICK

I have emphasized many times throughout this book the need to establish and nurture habits that serve you best. Hopefully, you have heeded this advice and implemented new habits. Perhaps you have established a predetermined waking time, followed by a workout routine, meditation or prayer, and a plan for the day. Or perhaps you have new nutritional practices that make you feel more alive and alert. You certainly don't want to lose these advantages as you transition out of warp speed. Take time to identify all the improvements that you want to retain as life settles into a new normal.

WEED YOUR GARDEN

Relationships, habits, ways of thinking, and distractions can all serve as weeds that choke the bountiful harvest you have planted and nurtured during your intensity push. You may have let some relationships wither during your time of intensity. These relationships may not serve you well as you move forward; they may threaten to pull you back into habits and lifestyles of the past. Decide which relationships need renewed attention and which ones you should let go of. Some relationships are lifelong, but you'll be better off without others.

Similarly, your old bad habits will be waiting for you right where you left them. As you slow down, don't fall back into old, unhelpful, or harmful routines. Remain keenly aware of the damage they caused and do not let them regain a foothold in your life.

STEP AWAY

As you approach the end of your intensity push, take a few days to step away from your life. Go somewhere by yourself—any place outside of town with few distractions can work well. Pick a hotel or a familiar Airbnb spot you like. Relax. Go for long walks, sit by the beach, or hike in the mountains. Mentally sort through what you want to take away from the intensity push.

WATCH YOUR SPEED

At this point, you have used the DISCIPLINE STRATEGY to reach a new plane of productivity and efficiency in your life. Now you must decide exactly what pace you want to maintain in the future. It likely won't be the same high level of intensity you maintained during this period of DISCIPLINE STRATEGY, but you probably don't want to return to your previous level of productivity, either.

Watch your speed closely as you throttle back. Even though you're slowing some things down, you don't want to hit the brakes entirely. You need to find the right cruising speed to ultimately carry you over the finish line. Then, as you get closer and closer to your goal, you'll probably find that you need to slow down a bit more. After all, a train can't go barreling into the train station at full speed!

I suggest you make your transition slowly and gradually, reducing a little bit of activity at a time, watching how things are progressing, and not losing sight of the goal. You still have things to do before you reach your goal, and you want to keep enough momentum going to ensure that you make it across the finish line.

NEW LIMITS

You should now have a new understanding of your limits and you've stretched them beyond what you thought was possible. Now it's time to take a moment to look around and evaluate how far you've come. We'll do that next.

──────── **TAKE IT FURTHER** ────────

This chapter includes one comprehensive worksheet to help you change gears to a high level of intensity. Please visit www. DISCIPLINESTRATEGY.com to access this worksheet and other resources. And be sure to understand your capacity for intensity and vulnerability to burnout by taking the MyPersonality Assessment.

Creating Intentional Life Imbalance Worksheet

The topic of life balance is a popular one these days. In this chapter, I have suggested the contrary point of life *imbalance*. However, I propose you do this with a conscious and intentional effort. Slashing and burning everything around you does not serve any purpose. This worksheet will help you identify and plan for the realignment of your priorities during this critical phase of the DISCIPLINE STRATEGY.

PHASE

4

CELEBRATE AND NURTURE CONTINUOUS GROWTH AND WELL-BEING

CHAPTER 9

NOTICE

"Sometimes we get so caught up in trying to accomplish something big that we fail to notice the little things that give life its magic."
—Anonymous

Our will to survive and find equilibrium is a great characteristic of humanity, but it is also a double-edged sword. We don't usually stay down for long after a serious misfortune, but neither do we stay up for long after a great success. Research indicates that people who suffer a significant personal tragedy, such as a disability or major life disappointment, often return to pre-tragedy levels of happiness within a few months. People who have not suffered a great tragedy find this hard to believe. It can be equally difficult to imagine how people who have something fantastic happen to them—like winning the lottery or achieving a huge life goal—find the exhilaration they feel in the moment of success fades quickly, returning them to their pre-fortune level of happiness.

In other words, everything normalizes over time. We all have a genetically predisposed level of well-being. No matter what happens to us—good or bad—we tend to return to that preprogrammed level.

Some unusual individuals, however, stride from one goal accomplishment to another, each time increasing their sense of well-being and motivation. Each successive goal is grander and moves them to a continually higher level. That is what I want for you—not a cycle of ups and downs, but a continuous upward spiral. You achieve this way of life by noticing the process, your internal dialogue, and your accomplishments. Just like a rock climber, you secure your position, survey your surroundings, and then start to move upward once again. Your destination is ever-increasing, lasting happiness and well-being.

Creating this kind of life is more challenging than you might think. At this point in the process, I want you to fight the tendency toward normalization. Notice how your efforts have resulted in reaching the goal you chose during the first step of the DISCIPLINE STRATEGY. You should integrate into your self-identity what you have learned and who you have become because of the accomplishment. As a result, you should be able to establish yourself on a higher plateau, ready for the next grand adventure.

To help with this, I'll refer to the Notice Worksheet several times in this chapter. This form, available at www.DISCIPLINESTRATEGY.com, is designed to guide you through the notice process, capture the lessons learned, and help you prepare to establish the next goal.

THE GROUND-LEVEL VIEW (WHAT THIS LOOKS LIKE IN REAL LIFE)

Lucy had spent eight years building a software business from scratch. As an MBA student at the University of Chicago, she was inspired by the idea of an online set of services that would simplify many of the administrative tasks required of small businesses. Even before graduation, she had a detailed business plan and had partnered with a computer science Ph.D. student named Taylor. Lucy was highly driven, mostly by the external pressures she had felt to succeed.

Lucy and Taylor worked well together. They each had a generous personality and reached mutual understanding easily. Together they built a solid software-as-a-service business. This type of business is built on annual software subscriptions and is typically quite profitable. Their success and growth were stunning.

During these intense eight years, Lucy's priorities gradually shifted, and she began planning for the next phase of her life. Lucy and Taylor reached the point where they were both ready to sell the business and move on to new adventures. There had been many unsolicited offers, and they knew that continuing to say no would eventually result in some of those rejected suitors starting their own similar operations.

So, in late 2017, they decided to market their business. This process was long and challenging. But with the help of an excellent business consultant and a team of lawyers, they finally sold the business on July 31, 2018. The closing was completed electronically, and Lucy verified the transfer of funds just prior to walking out the door that evening. She had logged into her investment account many times over the past eight years as she managed a growing portfolio of investments. On the previous day, her balance was $678,432. *Not bad*, she thought for a single 33-year-old entrepreneur. After the transaction closed, however, she found that her account balance now read $17,678,822!

The stunning thing to Lucy was that the $17 million windfall didn't leave her feeling any different. She walked outside to meet a friend, Michelle, who was taking her out to dinner to celebrate. As she got in the car, her friend asked her how the closing had gone. Lucy replied calmly, "Everything went smoothly. There were no last-minute issues, and I was able to verify that the funds were transferred to my account." Michelle congratulated Lucy, and they rode quietly for a couple of minutes as Michelle navigated the Chicago traffic.

During dinner, Lucy spoke a lot about what she could have done better, what she wished had been different, and some current life frustrations. Michelle, who knew Lucy quite well, stopped Lucy mid-sentence and shared her perspective: "Lucy, you have totally missed all you've accomplished. All you see are the negatives, the challenges, and what you *don't* like about this day. You need to notice everything you've done right, the self-discipline you have exercised, and the opportunities you have created for yourself and others."

Lucy was stunned. She realized that she had failed to notice the massive transformation that had occurred in her life over the past eight years. For so long, she had kept her nose to the grindstone, as her mother used to say, and she had rarely stopped to reflect on the journey and its many joys along the way.

Michelle suggested that Lucy take a moment to notice all that had gone right: the employees who loved the jobs Lucy had created, the small businesses that had benefited significantly from her software tools, and the numerous compelling options she now had in front of her. As they ordered another glass of wine and a rather decadent dessert, Lucy changed the lens through which she was viewing this accomplishment. And for the first time in a long while, she felt truly proud of herself.

THE CHALLENGES AND SOLUTIONS

The entire DISCIPLINE STRATEGY process is designed to guide you in the formation of goals that are self-determined, personally fulfilling, carefully planned, and deeply rewarding. It is also intended to help you avoid the numerous pitfalls that decades of research have identified. In this chapter, I want to stitch together several concepts that will help you hold on to the new plateau you reach with each goal.

You initially embraced the DISCIPLINE STRATEGY to accomplish an important life goal or solve a long-term challenge. As you find success with this process, you will begin to understand that life change is a never-ending journey. This step of noticing and locking in your new level of well-being is critical to long-term self-determination and an ever-improving you. So as we begin to bring the DISCIPLINE STRATEGY process in for a landing, let's keep our eyes on the following challenges in the notice stage:

- **FAILURE TO CELEBRATE:** Do not neglect the celebration. Once you have reached your goal, don't minimize it; celebrate it! In some cultures, celebration is encouraged; in others, it is viewed as immodest. To prevent normalization and build on your accomplishment, though, some form of celebration is crucial.

- **INTERNAL MISALIGNMENT:** The degree to which your goal has been consistent with your own internal compass will determine, to a surprising extent, how satisfied you are and whether you crash unexpectedly after its accomplishment. To build on your success and generate internal motivation for your next goal, you must find internal self-concordance.[22] This requires a continuous process of self-discovery and bold rejection of external forces.

- **SHORT-CIRCUITING FUTURE SUCCESS:** Success engenders future success—unless you choose to focus on negative self-talk, recast the past in a negative light, or choose not to celebrate your accomplishment. Here, you will learn how to put a capstone on your accomplishment in a way that brings one goal to a close while pointing you towards your next big win.

- **FORGETTING THE DETAILS:** Don't let yourself forget the details of how you accomplished your goal. Find creative ways to lock it into your memory and make it foundational to your

22 Kennon M. Sheldon and Andrew J. Elliot, "Goal Striving, Need Satisfaction, and Longitudinal Well-Being: The Self-Concordance Model," *Journal of Personality and Social Psychology*, 76(3), 1999, 482–497.

next goal. I love the creativity that some people can exhibit in finding ways to memorialize what they have done, and I'll help you come up with ideas of your own.

- **FAILURE TO LEVEL UP:** Whether or not you like video games, you've probably heard the concept of *leveling up*. In most video games, you first have to gain experience before you can master the level you're on. Once you do so, you can level up. It's important to note that you never *level down* after gaining valued experience, and you don't normally stay at a level you've already mastered. The only fulfilling direction to go is up! Life is the same way. To keep things interesting and stay in a growth mode, you must take your goals to the next level.

With these problem areas in mind, let's turn our eyes to some solutions to make sure we know how to accept our victory and set ourselves up for our next big win.

CHALLENGE: FAILURE TO CELEBRATE

Celebrating your achievement is a way to acknowledge what you have accomplished that increases happiness, self-confidence, and well-being. The more formal or ritualistic the celebration, the better.

When I completed my Ph.D., I had to decide whether to attend the university's *hooding ceremony*, the origins of which date back to the twelfth century, which includes a lot of pomp and circumstance. Given my incredibly busy schedule, I considered skipping the entire thing. However, I remembered how many times I'd advised other people not to skip the celebration when they achieve a big goal. So I went—and I'm so glad I did. It was a fantastic celebration, and I have a picture of the event hanging on my office wall to this day. It's amazing how much of a boost I get every time I see that picture. It's a lasting reminder that I set my sights on a big goal and overcame incredible obstacles to accomplish it.

In my earlier years, I used to plow through the accomplishments without ever stopping to notice or celebrate them. Missing those experiences was a huge mistake, and one I'll always regret. I don't want you to live with those kinds of regrets!

SOLUTION: FOLLOW TRADITION OR CREATE UNIQUELY MEANINGFUL CELEBRATIONS

Your celebration should be meaningful to you. Many key moments—such as my Ph.D. graduation—come with their own standard, traditional celebrations. In those situations, I highly recommend you follow tradition. Sure, it's easy to skip the celebration; our society has become cynical about such things, and we may feel like they're a waste of time. They're not. These are time-honored ways of remembering and noting big accomplishments. There is literally no downside here. Jump in and soak it up!

Other times, you'll need to exercise some creativity and create your own celebration. If a formal celebration for your accomplishment doesn't exist, then gather some friends, family, or go solo, but you need to celebrate in some way. Do something unique and memorable. In the aviation world, there is a tradition of cutting off the tail of your shirt and writing on it the date when you first flew an airplane by yourself. I know people who have had huge accomplishments but still consider that shirt-tail moment to be one of the most significant experiences of their lives. The way in which you memorialize or celebrate your accomplishment doesn't have to be elaborate or expensive; it just has to be meaningful to you.

CELEBRATION MATTERS

I don't want to beat a dead horse here, but I need you to understand why celebration matters. It's not just a time to bask in our egos and pat ourselves on our backs. Far from it! The act of celebrating actually creates physical changes in our brain chemistry, predisposing us to future success.

When we celebrate with authenticity, our brain responds with a biochemical change in dopamine levels. The act of celebrating signals your brain to release *feel-good* neurotransmitters. Not only does this bring on a sense of accomplishment, but it also trains our brains to value the actions we took to reach this moment. In this way, you encourage further accomplishment. Plus, celebration adds an emotionally charged event on top of the satisfaction of hitting a goal. Events that are more emotionally intense increase the level of detail stored in our memories and lead to better recall. In other words, celebrating solidifies the experience and makes a bigger imprint in your brain, which keeps things from simply going back to the way they were before the celebration. By hitting your goal and taking the time to celebrate, you are cementing a permanent change in your life.

Celebrating also encourages bonding in interpersonal relationships. When we celebrate together, a shift occurs in our hormonal system. If you celebrate with family, loved ones, or co-workers who supported you through your journey, you are also laying the groundwork, through bonding, for continued support as you move to the next goal.

Furthermore, when you celebrate, you solidify a new self-image and communicate it to others. The celebration marks the turning point when you became a new person. For example, many of us think of our high school graduation as a turning point. You walked across a stage, got a diploma, and changed from student to graduate. You became a different person at that point in time. The moment of celebration is the point where all your past work is recognized and integrated into your new identity. This is a powerful psychological tool that helps you modify your self-image.

CHALLENGE: INTERNAL MISALIGNMENT

It's time to calibrate your internal alignment system. The goal you accomplished was one you initiated, but were you doing it for the right reasons? Was it really *your* goal or something that your family or society pushed on you? It's sometimes difficult to sort this out. For example, I know a few doctors who went into medicine because that's what their parents wanted them to do. Or they had teachers who encouraged them in the sciences and they simply fell into medicine without much thought. It can be surprisingly difficult to discern *why* we pursue the things we do. And when we aren't sure if our hearts are *really* in it, we find ourselves confused about which goals are most closely aligned with our own desires.

SOLUTION: NOTE THE COMPASS DEVIATION

Hindsight is 20/20. It will be easier for you to determine the extent to which your goal was truly *yours* as you approach the finish line. With each accomplishment, assess how closely this activity aligned to your true self. Did achieving this goal make you *more* of who you really are? Did it bring you closer to who you ultimately want to become? Does completing this goal excite you, or do you feel surprisingly let down by the whole thing?

These inputs should inform your next goal. Perhaps this goal was *close* to your true interests, but you discovered a few tweaks were in order before you set out on your next adventure. Take the time to notice these things and apply them to your next goal pursuit. View your life as a series of goals that should—over time—more closely align with who you really are and what you really want. Your goals early in life will most likely be shaped more by personal assumptions and external expectations. As you grow older and accomplish these early goals, you should become more and more aware of where you *really* want to go. This upward improvement in goal alignment will occur only if you recalibrate, through intentional thought and self-assessment, after each goal is reached.

The DISCIPLINE STRATEGY Notice Worksheet, available for free at www.DISCIPLINESTRATEGY.com, walks you through a process of recalibrating and noting any deviations between your accomplishment and where you want to be. Capturing this deviation will help you plot the course to your next goal. The work-sheet asks three simple questions under "Internal Alignment":

1. To what degree do you feel like this accomplishment is aligned with who you really are?
2. If you do not have perfect alignment, can you identify what is missing or why there is a gap? In other words, what can you learn from this experience?
3. How would you shift your next goal in order to move to closer alignment with your core values, wants, desires, aspirations, and goals?

By considering and responding to these questions, you are prompting important mental considerations that are often overlooked. Our brains will attempt to justify things we do and normalize them. This makes it easy to convince yourself to accept your current situation as who you are or as the best you can do, rather than encouraging you to aim even higher. I want you to challenge yourself and examine what you have done to reveal deeper truths about your desires.

CHALLENGE: SHORT-CIRCUITING FUTURE SUCCESS

Noticing involves nurturing an upward spiral in your pursuit of happiness, personal growth, and accomplishment. Success should create the foundation for more success and happiness in the future, but it doesn't always work this way. You have to harvest your success, process it, and turn it into a solid foundation for future growth.

SOLUTION: ENGINEER YOUR NEXT STEP

Elon Musk, entrepreneur and tech CEO, once said, "People are mistaken when they think that technology just automatically improves. It does not automatically improve. It only improves if a lot of people work very hard to make it better, and actually it will, I think, by itself degrade."[23] Musk, of course, was talking about scientific technology, but I think this applies to our lives and our goals as well. You do not just automatically improve as you go forward; it takes a lot of work, self-awareness, and goal-engineering to build up rather than break down.

Your success should be a platform from which you launch into your next accomplishment. Twenty-five years of goal research by Edwin Locke and Gary Latham teach us several key points about goals.[24] You should allow this research to inform the manner and scope of your next goal:

- You perform better when you set a challenging goal than when you set a goal that is too easy or not well-defined.
- There is a positive linear relationship between the challenge the goal presents and how hard and effective you will work but only if you meet these conditions:
  - This is *your* goal and you are committed to it.
  - You are not missing some major required resource to reach the goal.
  - The goal is not in conflict with other goals or life standards you have set for yourself.
- Understand that when you set the goal you are defining a gap between where you are now and where you want to be. This will create some discomfort but think of it as *constructive discontent*.

You must carefully engineer, based on insights from past accomplishments, a new goal that is more precisely defined and more difficult. Bringing Musk's statement into our goal discussion, you'll need to work very hard to make *yourself* better.

23 Justin Bariso, "Elon Musk Just Gave Some Brilliant Career Advice. Here It Is in 1 Sentence," *Inc.com*, May 8, 2017, https://www.inc.com/justin-bariso/elon-musk-just-gave-some-brilliant-career-advice-here-it-is-in-1-sentence.html.
24 E.A. Locke and G.P. Latham, "New Directions in Goal-Setting Theory," *Current Directions in Psychological Science*, 15(5), 2006, 265–268.

Building on success is not automatic; it must be engineered. The Notice Worksheet helps you brainstorm ideas for your next pursuit. This activity will capture the flurry of ideas that often burst forth at a time of goal accomplishment. Don't think of this as a decision point for your next goal; that will come when you return to the beginning of the DISCIPLINE STRATEGY to make the decision on your next step. Instead, think of this as an opportunity to set some new ground rules for your next goal-development process.

This part of the Notice Worksheet asks four key questions:

1. Where do you need to focus your energies in order to expand your capabilities, skills, or education?
2. Where did you feel weak or lacking through the goal-accomplishment process?
3. What strengths surprised you that you can leverage better going forward?
4. Who turned out to be a key resource that you had not expected?

Do not lose track of the lessons gained during the journey to this accomplishment. You have no doubt grown tremendously and become a new and better version of yourself. In addition, during that growth period, you inevitably perceived opportunities for further improvement, discovered strengths that could be applied to the next goal pursuit, and saw people come into your life whom you would never have anticipated but who played a key role in some way. Capture all this. You're a goal engineer, and these will be the raw materials and tools with which you build your next success.

CHALLENGE: FORGETTING THE DETAILS

Noticing means not letting your accomplishments normalize. What you have achieved is extraordinary. A goal should transform you into a different person. You had to become more capable, disciplined, educated, and experienced to reach your goal. This process actually creates a better, more refined version of you. However, decay is the natural order of the universe, so you have to actively fight it.

SOLUTION: PAINT A NEW SELF-IDENTITY

Forget the old you. I want you to redefine your identity. I am not talking about unsubstantiated self-esteem building, which does nothing for you. What I have in mind is affirming, based on facts and your proven abilities and accomplishments. This will result in increased self-efficacy.

There is some debate over where the real value lies in goal achievement. Is it in accomplishing the thing you set out to do, or is the value more in the growth you experienced while pursuing your goal? I believe the best answer is an 80/20 split: 80 percent of the value is in the personal change that occurs and 20 percent is in the goal itself. That's mainly because the changes that occur in your attitude, nature, and character will stay with you for life. To maximize this value, document and build upon these changes. Identifying the positive changes, writing them down, and integrating them into your self-image locks in the value and prepares you to set an appropriately difficult new goal afterward.

Look back at where you were when you made the decision to pursue this goal. Use the Notice Worksheet to record where you started in terms of your strengths and capabilities and where you wound up. Record a positive statement that summarizes your new strengths and captures the improvement. Mark the traits you feel would be good to build on when setting your next goal. Below is an example from the story about Lucy at the beginning of this chapter:

Lucy's example is interesting. Even though her accomplishment was incredible, she walked away from it with an unexpected mixture of emotions. Now, having identified new strengths that she wants to build on, she will be better equipped to plan for her next life goal.

NOTICE WORKSHEET
LOCK IT IN

DISCIPLINE STRATEGY
THE SCIENTIFIC ROADMAP FOR CHANGE

You need to notice the growth and improvements made during the accomplishment of this goal. Identify personal characteristics of the "old me" and how they have improved in the "new me." Indicate in the checkbox those strengths you want to build on for your next goal.

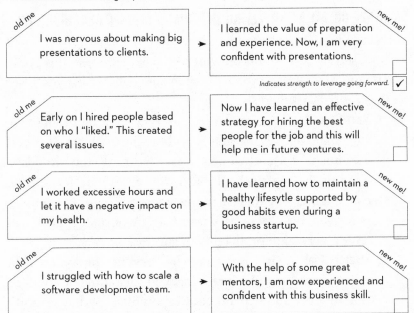

old me
I was nervous about making big presentations to clients.

new me!
I learned the value of preparation and experience. Now, I am very confident with presentations.

Indicates strength to leverage going forward. ✓

old me
Early on I hired people based on who I "liked." This created several issues.

new me!
Now I have learned an effective strategy for hiring the best people for the job and this will help me in future ventures.

old me
I worked excessive hours and let it have a negative impact on my health.

new me!
I have learned how to maintain a healthy lifesytle supported by good habits even during a business startup.

old me
I struggled with how to scale a software development team.

new me!
With the help of some great mentors, I am now experienced and confident with this business skill.

The process of learning and growing never stops. But to avoid falling backwards, you need to lock in the strengths and integrate them into your future goal setting. Unless you are purposeful about identifying and planning to utilize your newfound strengths, they will fade. Use the worksheet to document the most significant changes you observed in your strengths.

CHALLENGE: FAILURE TO LEVEL UP

In this step of the DISCIPLINE STRATEGY, you have celebrated, completed an internal realignment, noted the positive aspects of your success, and locked it in. Now it is time to level up. Some people lose focus and slip backwards with no sense of direction after a big accomplishment. The DISCIPLINE STRATEGY is designed to help you avoid those pitfalls. To keep your internal motivation high and build goal by goal to an even higher level, you must transfer your momentum to the next endeavor.

SOLUTION: CREATE A COMPELLING, INTERNALLY ALIGNED NEXT BIG THING

You should never rest too long in the harbor of accomplishment without setting your sights on your next destination. At this point, I want you to sketch out three possible big goals, which you'll see on the Notice Worksheet:

1. **Next-Step Goal:** A next-step goal is a logical, progressive step that follows the goal you have just achieved. If you are finishing a bachelor's degree, the next step would be a job or graduate school. Next-step goals may feel a little challenging, but they fit with where you are and will be perceived by others as reasonable. A next-step goal will have a very high probability of success.

2. **Stretch Goal:** A stretch goal pushes beyond the logical next step for most people. It requires you to assume you will be able to grow and expand your capabilities, perhaps significantly. It should feel uncomfortable. You may not be able to see the path or believe you have the capability to reach this goal. A stretch goal will require a major research effort to identify potential paths to the goal, plus significant effort to build new capabilities. Stretch goals can create a huge amount of motivation when closely aligned with who you are and your internal compass.

3. **No-Fear, No-Hesitation Goal:** On May 25, 1961, then U.S. president John F. Kennedy delivered a famous speech in which he stated, "This nation should commit itself to achieving the goal, before the decade is out, of landing a man on the moon and returning him safely to the Earth." This speech introduced the concept of a *moonshot* into our vocabulary. A moonshot is at the upper end of the no-fear, no-hesitation

goal spectrum. On the lower end, you would find a goal that exceeds anything to which you can currently see a clear path. These goals are created when you drop all the perceived internal and external constraints—even constraints that seem absolutely unavoidable.

These types of goals are mind-expanding exercises. Yes, you may actually decide to pursue one of these goals, but even if you don't, the thought experiment can point you in a new direction. You will certainly discover new thoughts and previously unleashed ideas. Just remember that you're only sketching these ideas out at this point. Now is not the time to set them in stone; you'll do that later as you restart the DISCIPLINE STRATEGY process for your new goals. For now, simply extract all the insights you can from what you've already accomplished.

LOOKING BEHIND AND POINTING AHEAD

The notice step is your time to look back a bit and reflect on what you've done, where you've come from, how you've grown, and who you are becoming. Nothing brings sharper focus to these things than the successful completion of a big goal! This is a critically important step not just for wrapping up your current goal but for forecasting you next goals, as well. Noticing these things points the way ahead; it shows you what you're equipped to do next and, more importantly, what you *want* to do next. Soon you will be ready to begin the more intense process of deciding which goal to adopt as you start the DISCIPLINE STRATEGY again.

———— TAKE IT FURTHER ————

The Notice Worksheet, mentioned a few times throughout this chapter, is a key piece of the DISCIPLINE STRATEGY process. If you haven't done so already, be sure to download it now at www.DISCIPLINESTRATEGY.com.

Notice Worksheet

The Notice Worksheet helps you to commit to celebration, assess alignment of your current goal with your internal desires, begin the engineering process for your next goal, document and lock in your areas of personal growth, and inspire you to level up. Use this worksheet as you approach your goal or immediately after you have attained it. This will serve as a foundation for starting the DISCIPLINE STRATEGY with your next goal.

CHAPTER 10

ENJOY

"Accomplishment only has meaning in a complete frame-work of nurturing well-being and happiness."
—TIMOTHY L. COOMER, PH.D.

The great Earl Nightingale, to whom I referred earlier in this book, challenged my entire understanding of success many years ago. In his wonderful presentation of *The Strangest Secret*, he defined success in an entirely new way. He said, "Success is the progressive realization of a worthy ideal [or goal]." Notice he didn't say success only comes when you *accomplish* your goal; rather, success comes through the *progressive realization* of your goal. That means you become a success the moment you clearly define a worthy goal and start working toward it. Therefore, I have good news for you: you're *already* a success! Of course, I want you to see your goal through to completion and accomplishing your goal will add an entirely new dimension of joy and satisfaction to your life, but the good news about this final step, enjoy, is that you don't have to wait until the very end of the process. You can begin *enjoying* your success today!

And so, as we bring the DISCIPLINE STRATEGY process to a close in this chapter, I want you to learn why taking a moment to enjoy your success is so important. Plus, I'll give you an inside look into the life of one couple who has worked the DISCIPLINE STRATEGY process from start to finish and found unbelievable joy on the other side. That can—and should—be you too.

THE POWER OF PERMA

If the act of working toward your goals makes you feel joyful and successful (and it should), then just think about how over-the-top joyful and successful you'll feel when you actually cross the finish line. I've spent my entire adult life working toward some enormous goals. I've been tired, frustrated, stressed, and sometimes downright terrified. But I've also been thrilled, exhilarated, energized, and completely satisfied. Why? It's because goals have brought meaning and focus to my life, and they've prevented me from living a haphazard, accidental existence. They've always been sitting there, just above the horizon, pulling me ever-onward. That's an incredible feeling—especially when I absolutely crush a big goal I've been working on for months or years.

As big a fan of goals as I clearly am, I know that achieving your goals has little meaning if it doesn't result in increased well-being and happiness. If you can't enjoy the fruits of your labor, if you can't be proud of what you've accomplished, then what's the point in having goals at all? So my last bit of advice is pretty straightforward: enjoy your life and accomplishments!

The DISCIPLINE STRATEGY is designed to nurture all the drivers of your well-being. It supports you through the goal-achievement process and is the perfect roadmap for change. Because the DISCIPLINE STRATEGY teaches you how to create a customized, self-directed plan, it should enable you to increase your level of positive emotion, build healthy relationships, and find meaning—all while accomplishing your goals. Those are wonderful outcomes!

But how can we measure the joy we're looking for? How does one quantify a sense of well-being? It certainly doesn't come from simply conceiving a new goal such as "Be happier" or "Find joy." That may sound silly to you, but I'm always surprised when people make the pursuit of joy or happiness into a goal. Yes, it's a wonderful outcome, but joy itself isn't something you can target and happiness isn't a destination. Rather, it's the natural result of accomplishing something else. Joy and well-being aren't once-and-for-all, take-it-or-leave it goals; they're baked into *every single goal* you'll ever work toward. If your goal is to earn a Ph.D., the outcome of achieving that goal will be a Ph.D. *and* joy. If your goal is to start a new business with $10 million in gross revenue, the outcome of achieving that goal will be a new business with $10 million in gross revenue *and* joy. No, I'm not saying that degrees and wealth are the keys to happiness; I'm simply saying that you can't accomplish big goals like this without also getting a major boost to your sense of well-being. The key to finding this joy is to know where to look.

My research into personality modeling, performance, and goal theory led me to the world of positive psychology as defined by Professor Martin Seligman, who is often referred to as the "father of positive psychology." In his 2011 book, *Flourish*, Dr. Seligman builds on decades of research to introduce the building blocks of well-being. These building blocks are represented by the acronym PERMA. When our work and goal-accomplishment take these five things into account, and when we are able to prioritize these five things even while we're focused on big goals, the result is increased well-being and satisfaction across the board. The acronym PERMA represents five aspects of well-being, which are:

- **P**ositive Emotion
- **E**ngagement
- **R**elationships
- **M**eaning
- **A**ccomplishment

I'll take just a moment to explain each of these in the hopes that you'll use what you've learned from the DISCIPLINE STRATEGY to harvest a rich crop of well-being and satisfaction from your successful goal achievement.

I will caution you up front, though, that you must be intentional about mining for this feel-good gold. If you're not, you may be surprised to find feelings of depression and unfulfillment creeping into your post-accomplishment mindset. But by understanding PERMA and keeping these five things in mind throughout your goal-accomplishment journey, you can avoid that trap and lay the foundation for a life of ever-growing happiness and well-being.

P – POSITIVE EMOTION

Prior to the positive psychology movement, the field of psychology focused primarily on relieving suffering and minimizing negative emotions. Today, we understand that psychology isn't just about relieving pain; it's about fostering a healthy, positive mindset and outlook on life. In other words, an emphasis on positive emotion should be more about boosting what's good than it is about fixing what's been hurt. But doing this isn't as easy as it might sound. Nurturing positive emotions doesn't consist of simply faking a smile or repeating a few positive phrases; it involves a major shift in habits and in how one sees the world.

Positive emotions are motivating. We often seek experiences that make us feel happy, excited, encouraged, and enlivened. Positive emotions have been shown to increase health, broaden one's perspective, improve relationships, and even extend life expectancy. Therefore, even though you'll spend days, weeks, and months intensely focused on your goal, you cannot allow yourself to be wholly consumed by it. As I stressed in chapter 8, Intensify, you can't completely cut *everything* else out of your life while working toward your goal. You need to make time for some rest and relaxation. Burnout will always remain a threat to your goal-accomplishment and well-being, so you must guard against it by nurturing positive emotions and making room for fun in your life.

I'll add another warning here: if there's ever a time when the pursuit of your goal is adding nothing but stress, pain, fear, anxiety, and doubt to your life, take that as a sign to step back and reexamine what you're doing and why you're doing it. Yes, accomplishing your big goal will be hard work, but that doesn't mean it should be constant drudgery. If you end up hating what you're doing halfway through your goal process, go back through the loop process (chapter 7) and figure out what needs to change. Achieving your goal should be a joy; if it's not, something's wrong. Don't let a blind commitment to your goal wreck your life.

E – ENGAGEMENT

Engagement is commonly described as being in the *flow*, or that unique state of being where you seem to be fully one with the activity you're engaged in. When you're engaged, you are not consciously *thinking* about what you are doing; rather, you are *part* of what you are doing. You lose track of time, concentration is complete and almost effortless, and your worries disappear. It's like a surgeon who is deeply engaged in performing a serious operation. A ten-hour, nonstop surgical procedure that requires the surgeon to be on his feet and completely focused in a life-or-death situation sounds impossible, and yet this happens every day in every hospital around the world. Many doctors I know have told me how a five-hour surgery seems to fly by. In fact, some even comment on how surprised they are at the end of a procedure to realize how long they've been on their feet and focused on such important, finely detailed work.

This level of engagement or flow is achieved when you are using an elevated level of skill to do a challenging task. I feel it when I am landing my airplane or engaged in a complex mathematical modeling effort. Others will find flow in their painting, gardening, writing, or playing sports. Researchers have examined this state of consciousness and described it as qualitatively different from our normal state. The more you can engineer flow experiences in your life, the greater your sense of well-being will be. These are the times when you know, deep in your spirit, that you are doing exactly what you were designed to do. There's no feeling quite like it.

R – RELATIONSHIPS

Research scientists, counselors, and the average person on the street all agree that vibrant and healthy relationships with other people improve happiness and well-being. Multiple research studies over the years have shown that positive relationships with one's spouse, family, and close friends are the strongest predictor of life satisfaction. The point is, *relationships matter*. In fact, when we are at risk of becoming isolated, our brains trigger a pain response. We were created to seek social connections, and we feel noticeable pain when isolated from them. That's why I warned you not to completely cut off your family and friends during your intensity push (chapter 8). I don't know anyone who wants to get to the end of their goal journey and find that they've accomplished their goal but lost their marriage, friends, and connection with their children. That certainly doesn't sound like *success* to me.

The good news is that positive relationships can be intentionally nurtured. Each of us has many different types of relationships. In this effort, you will focus on your bonded relationships (i.e., spouse, life partner, or significant other) and close friends. If, in the course of working toward your goal, you start feeling completely isolated from other people—especially your most important relationships—take that as a sign to take a break from your work and reconnect with your loved ones. Whether it's a short weekend trip or just a night out with your spouse, don't be scared to sacrifice a little bit of productivity for the sake of your relationships. It's a worthy trade, and one that will pay huge dividends in the long run.

M - MEANING

Having a purpose and doing things that give meaning to your life represent another key component of well-being. For millions of people, a religious commitment provides this sense of ultimate purpose and direction. If that's a foreign concept for you, I encourage you to explore the faith-based part of your life. Deep, spiritual connections bring an entirely new depth and meaning to your life. It is a wonderful reminder that there's more to our lives than *just* our lives.

Whether spirituality is a part of your life or not, you will still find meaning in your many other roles as a husband or wife, son or daughter, parent, professional, member of your community, and so on. Volunteer endeavors are an especially powerful way to make a positive impact on others and find a new dimension of fulfillment you may have never known. Ultimately, we cannot avoid the truth that doing things just for ourselves does not provide the deep fulfillment that gives our lives meaning. So if you accomplish your big goal and still feel a void in your life, I encourage you to find new ways to add value to someone else's life. In doing so, you could very well fill the hole in your own life.

A - ACCOMPLISHMENTS

You probably bought and read this book because you were looking for a clear path to accomplish some grand goal in your life. And, to be honest, there are few joys in life sweeter than the sense of accomplishment that comes from achieving a hard-fought goal. Once you get a taste, you'll want to experience it more and more. It becomes a deeply engrained and much-loved aspect of your personal sense of well-being.

As we discussed in the previous chapter, it is crucial to set aside time to celebrate our big wins. It's not just a high-five or emotional thrill; basking in our victories changes our hearts and minds in a fundamental—even biochemical—manner. It equips us to keep fighting, keep pushing, and keep pursuing newer and bigger goals. You should *never* stop pursuing accomplishments. In fact, doing so might kill you! One recent research study showed a spike in death rates that correlated with a spike in retirement at age sixty-two.[25] Apparently, age alone isn't the biggest health challenge you may find in retirement; it may be a lack of clear goals and sense of accomplishment.

The moment you stop setting and working toward big goals is the moment you start to fade away both mentally and physically. In the early days of World War II, Winston Churchill spoke these words: "Never give in, never give in, never, never, never, never— in nothing, great or small, large or petty—never give in except to convictions of honor and good sense."[26] A great sense of accomplishment isn't just our reward for a job well done; it's our fuel for the next goal we're sure to attack with excellence. As Churchill stated later in the same speech, "We can be sure that we have only to persevere to conquer."

GUIDE TO HAPPINESS AND WELL-BEING

While I broke down each component of PERMA, I strongly encourage you to download the detailed DISCIPLINE STRATEGY Guide to Happiness and Well-being from www. DISCIPLINESTRATEGY.com. In that pack of worksheets, I provide an individual form to walk you through each piece of the PERMA puzzle. If you've followed me this far into your goal-accomplishment journey, you should trust me enough to see this thing all the way through! I'll mention this activity again in the Take It Further section at the end of this chapter.

25 M.D. Fitzpatrick and T.J. Moore, "The mortality effects of retirement: Evidence from Social Security eligibility at age 62," *Journal of Public Economics* Volume 157, January 2018, 121–137.

26 Winston Churchill, "Never Give In, Never, Never, Never," (presentation, Harrow School, October 29, 1941), https://www.nationalchurchillmuseum.org/never-give-in-never-never-never.html.

THE GROUND-LEVEL VIEW (WHAT THIS LOOKS LIKE IN REAL LIFE)

Throughout this book, I've given you a ground-level view of each step in the DISCIPLINE STRATEGY process. I've done this to put a real-world face on what might otherwise be a heady, philosophical conversation. But I hope by now you understand that goals don't simply take place in the mind; goals are *actions*. To bring all these individual principles into focus, I'd like to conclude this book with one final ground-level view. I should point out, however, that this is not a composite story with the names and places changed to protect the innocent. This is, in fact, a real couple who clearly demonstrate the power of a decision and the benefits of positive life change. And, instead of just giving you part of the story as I've done in the ground-level view for other chapters, I'll use this case study to show what the *entire* process looks like in real life.

As you'll see, the process isn't as clear-cut in practice as it is in theory. I'm sure you've found in your own pursuits that the steps in the DISCIPLINE STRATEGY often overlap as you adapt to real-world demands and surprises. That's okay. The point isn't to work this program perfectly; the point is to conceive, create, work toward, and accomplish your worthy goals. Don't worry if a few of the steps happen simultaneously or even slightly out of order. My goal here has been to simply provide a clear framework you can apply to your goal pursuits. Of course, this isn't a license to throw this whole process out the window! I still believe the DISCIPLINE STRATEGY process is the *best* way to advance toward your goal, so I encourage you to stick to it as closely as possible.

Now, with that disclaimer out of the way, I'd like to introduce you to Paul and Karen. We'll walk through their DISCIPLINE STRATEGY story piece by piece. As we go, I'll call out which steps they're covering in the DISCIPLINE STRATEGY model. For reference, here are the four phases and ten steps we've discussed throughout this book:

Phase 1: *Choosing the Destination and Preparing for the Journey*
D – Decide
I – Investigate
S – Sort

Phase 2: *Create the Roadmap and Begin the Journey*
C – Conceive
I – Implement
P – Persevere

Phase 3: *Perfect and Intensify your Efforts*
L – Loop
I – Intensify

Phase 4: *Celebrate and Nurture Continuous Growth and Well-being*
N – Notice
E – Enjoy

With that, let's get to know Paul and Karen.

STARTING POSITIONS

She waited until she reached the parking lot to cry. In the spring of 2005, at the age of thirty-six, Karen was a bubbly, outgoing woman who was engaged to the love of her life. She had also just received a painful jolt of truth at a doctor's appointment. When she stepped onto the scales, she weighed 271 pounds. It shouldn't have been a shock—Karen knew she was overweight—but something about that number jarred her. Her fiancé weighed 303 pounds and, if she didn't do something soon, her weight would soon match his. Many emotions flooded Karen's brain: embarrassment, fear, despair. The number on the scale shouted in a voice that couldn't be denied and she felt convicted by her lack of discipline. She was out of control.

Karen had been overweight as a child and, though she was on the pep squad in high school, she wasn't athletic. As an adult, she partied hard and enjoyed life in abundance but, after a failed marriage and joining a new church in her community, she was ready to reevaluate her choices. Looking back, Karen says she didn't *need* a man in her life—but she *wanted* one. She longed for someone to share both the burdens of a stressful job and the simple joys of everyday life. She tried online dating and soon met her future husband. They married in December 2005.

Paul was a telecommunications specialist and a twenty-year Air Force veteran. He also loved to eat, and it showed on his 6 ft. 1 inch frame. Although Paul had played recreational sports in his younger years, he admits he struggled even then to keep his weight in check. In the military, Paul was forced to participate in a diet and fitness regimen designed to help overweight service-members reach optimal weight and fitness standards. Now, newly married, Paul was bothered by his weight ... but not enough to do much about it.

PHASE I: DECIDE, INVESTIGATE, SORT

Already twice divorced, Paul's marriage to Karen was an exciting new start. They shared similar personalities, loved to be around people, and were both committed to their church. Life was good, but Karen's heart was heavy. She wanted to lose weight. She wanted to be strong and healthy. She wanted to be someone others valued as a witness to discipline and self-control. The doctor's scales proved otherwise. She was not the person she wanted to be. Standing in the parking lot at her doctor's office, tears streaming down her face, Karen made a decision.

Her first act after her face-off with the doctor's scales was a trip to the bookstore. She bought *The South Beach Diet* and started following its program by tracking her food choices and walking. She didn't know anyone athletic—her friends were all sedentary—but Karen's outgoing personality served her well in her search for people who could help her attain her goals. Her new health-minded friends helped her sort through the mountains of nutrition information (and misinformation) she had discovered, and she began to catch a vision for a new way of life—a life that wasn't only marked by weight loss but by actually getting off the couch and participating in some of the activities her fitter friends enjoyed. But how?

PHASE 2: CONCEIVE, IMPLEMENT, PERSEVERE

She found a walking buddy and together they signed up for the 2006 Country Music Half Marathon in Nashville. It was a challenging first goal, to be sure, but the casual walking pace and friendly conversations she enjoyed while walking made it seem well within reach. When Karen and her friend crossed the finish line at their walking pace, however, Karen felt something new stir within her. There was something in the thrill of the race environment and the enthusiasm of the crowd that sparked a new goal—a much more difficult goal—in her mind. So as she walked across the finish line of her 2006 half marathon, Karen conceived her first big fitness goal: the following year, 2007, she would *run* that race.

A friend introduced her to the Jeff Galloway method of adding walk segments into the run. Karen's first attempt at the run/walk approach meant walking one minute and running one minute, but she found she could only manage thirty seconds of the run. This only fueled her determination. Paul countered that a run/walk was not really running (a comment that resulted in the first big fight of their relationship), but Paul had to admit something positive and exciting was happening in Karen. She was down to 225 pounds, then 200. Motivated by his wife's success, Paul decided he better get moving too.

They were each even more ambitious as a team. They found a running store that supported group runs. Even though it was twenty miles from their home and the runs were short, they committed to being there. Their circle of friends now consisted of athletes and running enthusiasts. Karen and Paul had changed their lifestyle, routine, food choices, and friend group, and they were happy. Even though they hadn't accomplished their biggest goal, they were allowing themselves to enjoy their journey. But life wasn't done with its challenges.

In 2007, Paul and Karen were in the process of adopting a child but, after four months of having the child in their home, the baby's grandparents successfully petitioned the court for custody. Karen also began having serious knee issues that forced her to stop running. She was able to complete her second half marathon that year, but she wasn't able to run the whole course as planned. Rather, she used the same run/walk method to cross the finish line—in no small amount of pain, I might add. These significant losses, plus work stress and the loss of a parent, took a toll. Karen's weight climbed to over 200 pounds again. The joy and excitement she had started to feel as an athlete were fading fast—as was her general sense of well-being.

That's when a wise friend suggested Karen try swimming. That would give her an outlet for her athletic aspirations while also giving her knee time to heal, and it would be a healthy way to deal with the stress that had crept back into her life. Always comfortable in the water and ready to return to her fledgling athletic goals, Karen followed his advice. Over time, her weight stabilized and her mood improved as she devoted more time to swimming and allowed herself to start dreaming of new physical fitness goals. Soon after, she had the conversation that would change everything.

PHASE 3: LOOP, INTENSIFY

It was casual enough. Karen and a friend were just talking about a race the friend had just completed—a triathlon that combined swimming, biking, and running. Karen was intrigued by the triathlon concept and wondered if she was "tough enough" to get through one. That goal would have seemed impossible just a year earlier, but now, it didn't seem so crazy. After all, she was already swimming and had started running again after getting injections in her knee. Biking would be new to her, but it wouldn't be a huge strain on her knee and seemed easier than the swimming and running she was already doing every week. Maybe a triathlon was the natural progression of her initial fitness goals. As she looped back around to review what all she'd already done and what she really wanted to accomplish, a triathlon seemed to make sense. Plus, it wasn't a completely new goal; it fit well into her progress up to that point and gave her a slightly bigger target to shoot for. She was in.

To her surprise and delight, Paul was on board too. He signed up for the Cedars of Lebanon Sprint Triathlon (300-yard swim, 16.5-mile bike, 5K run) and Karen committed to the Ramblin' Rose Women's Only Sprint Triathlon (250-yard swim, 8-mile bike, 2-mile run). Triathlons were much more exciting and challenging than running races and both Karen and Paul were hooked. They continually reviewed and refined their fitness goals, and they weren't scared to bring surprisingly new levels of intensity to their progress. Before long, they joined a triathlon team and signed up for longer and harder races as they started focusing on their ultimate goals: a full Ironman for Paul and a Half Ironman for Karen. (Note: A full Ironman is comprised of a 2.4-mile swim, a 112-mile bike ride, and a 26.2-mile run for a combined 140.6 miles. A Half Ironman cuts each of those distances by half for a combined 70.3 miles. Both are the top endurance races of the multisport hallmark known as triathlon.)

PHASE 4: NOTICE, ENJOY

In October 2013, Paul finished Ironman Louisville, the date of which just happened to coincide with his fiftieth birthday. In 2014, he followed with Ironman Chattanooga. Then, in November 2016, Karen finished her first Half Ironman in North Carolina. The sad, depressed, embarrassed, overweight patient who cried as she left a doctor's appointment years earlier was now a fit, healthy triathlete with a new sense of well-being. She had done it.

Of course, none of these successes mean their weight struggles are over. They still have to face their food demons every day, but now they do so with ingenuity and discipline. They track food choices using a popular fitness and nutrition tracking app on their phones. They keep before and after photos to remind themselves how much they've accomplished. They have a large wall calendar on which they give themselves either a colorful smiley face (signifying good eating choices) or a black X (signifying unhealthy choices) every day. And they keep each other accountable and motivated by signing up for races up to a year in advance so that they are always training for something tangible.

But Paul and Karen take it a step further. They feel a keen obligation to help others move from an unhealthy, sedentary life to a life of fitness and energy. Paul is now on the board of the triathlon team. Together, he and Karen lead running groups, long bike rides, and open water swims. They invite new triathletes to train with them to learn the intricacies of the sport. Their positivity is infectious, and their natural friendliness inspires a large number of would-be triathletes. Most importantly, they don't shy away from sharing their story. It is always in the forefront of their minds—how far they've come and how much further they still want to go.

NEXT STEPS

So what's next for Paul and Karen? It's whatever goal they set their minds to. Not only do they know a process that will lead them to success, they also have a history of success to look back on. They will never lose sight of where they came from, and they will use that history and their goal-accomplishment victories to drive them to ever-evolving levels of success. And along with that success comes a sense of achievement and well-being neither Paul nor Karen had ever known. They no longer see themselves as victims of obesity and poor health. Instead, they see themselves as they truly are: strong, powerful, overcomers who have what it takes to set huge goals and see them through to completion.

IT'S YOUR TURN

This book has given you ten steps that guide you from the point of decision to accomplishing positive life change. Perhaps you've read this book over the course of many months, focusing on each step as you've worked toward your goal. Or maybe you've read this book in one sitting, trying to get a process in mind before actually taking your first step. The truth is, it doesn't matter which path you took. The only thing that matters as we wrap up the DISCIPLINE STRATEGY is what you believe about your ability to create positive life change. Do you feel empowered to set big goals? Do you feel equipped to work toward them, seeing them through to completion? Are you prepared to actually enjoy the fruit of your labor, giving yourself permission to feel good about what you've done and the person you have become?

I hope so. As I've said, this book isn't just theory; it's based on research, experimentation, and a lot of trial and error. Oftentimes, I was the guinea pig for the experimentation! I've been blessed by some really big wins, and I've been challenged by some really big losses. That's how life works. Sometimes you get exactly what you want, sometimes you don't get it at all, and sometimes—*sometimes*—you get so much more than you ever expected. That's what I want for you: a life filled with powerful and intentional decisions for life change that result in ever-increasing happiness and well-being.

I've given you a system that empowers you to design the life you desire. Now, it's your turn. Are you going to return to where you were before you picked up this book, or are you going to do something amazing? You now have a system that works. If you add to that a passion for accomplishing something great, I promise, you'll do more, go further, and make a bigger difference than you ever imagined. And I can't wait to hear all about it!

————TAKE IT FURTHER————

Now that you have a good understanding of the DISCIPLINE STRATEGY, you can use your new knowledge and skills to implement strategies that increase happiness and well-being. That positive emotional state will in turn improve your intrinsic motivation to make another decision, bigger and bolder than before, that will help you grow personally, serve others, and change the world. The worksheets mentioned here will help you do just that. You can download these forms for free at www.DISCIPLINESTRATEGY.com.

DISCIPLINE STRATEGY Guide to Happiness and Well-being

The Guide to Happiness and Well-being is a pack of worksheets designed to walk you through each piece of the PERMA puzzle. In these forms, you'll work through exercises to help you build positive emotion, engagement, relationships, meaning, and accomplishments. I encourage you to use these worksheets to carefully consider each component of PERMA and design a plan to nurture your happiness and well-being.

ACKNOWLEDGMENTS

No one writes a book without a lot of support and understanding from those around them. First, and most important, I thank my wife, Sandy, for her unwavering support, encouragement, and love. Sandy is a living example of what I teach in this book, and she inspires me every day as I watch her live her life as a writer and entrepreneur. I am a better person and writer because of the thirty-five years we have journeyed through life together. Second, my father, the wisest man I have ever known, has supported me in every major life decision, business startup, and success. He made the dream of entrepreneurship a goal I could grasp. He provided guidance in those moments when it was most critical. I am forever thankful for his giving heart and incredible wisdom. Third, I am blessed with a mom who has encouraged me and believed in everything I have ever done from the day I was born. As a young person, I benefited from many hours of her listening and quietly advising me as I attempted to sketch out a future for myself. The gift of total love and acceptance from my mom laid a foundation of self-confidence that has been vital to my success.

I am blessed with four wonderful children: Shawn, Ryan, Seth, and Nick. Each of them has provided valued feedback concerning this book. Their perspective as young adults (ages 20 to 30) has greatly improved this book. My greatest blessing in life is the opportunity I have been given to be their father. I love you all more than you will ever know.

Writing a book is the result of having built knowledge and experience and then finding a way to share insights with others. Many people influenced me along my academic journey, but two were most important. First, I thank Dr. Richard Duvall, Ph.D. Dr. Duvall was my boss at my first job after graduating from business school. He showed me the incredible value of doctoral-level education and taught me this, "We can do anything we set our minds to if we are given enough time." I cannot fully express how that belief has helped me reach past my comfort zone during the past thirty years. Dr. Duvall inspired me to complete a Ph.D. later in life. Second, I thank Dr. J. Craig Wallace, Ph.D., who served as the chairman of my dissertation committee at Oklahoma State University. Dr. Wallace facilitated the fastest period of academic and personal growth I have ever experienced. He ignited within me a passion for personality modeling and research. He showed me how to digest massive quantities of research and then to translate that knowledge into useful information that could be communicated to others. I do not believe I could have found a better academic mentor within any university on the planet.

This book benefited from two excellent editors. First, during the original writing of the first draft, I was guided by Dr. Bruce Barron. Dr. Barron showed great patience with me as a new writer, provided excellent editorial assistance, and made qualitative suggestions beyond editing of my early writings. Second, my publisher, Forefront Books, introduced me to Allen Harris. Allen is a highly experienced editor who dove into my manuscript, made significant suggestions for the structure and presentation of the content, and greatly improved the final manuscript. And to my publisher, Jonathan Merkh, whose vast experience and wisdom far exceeded anything I could have hoped for when I first set my sights on writing a book. I cannot thank Jonathan enough for his belief in me and my book, and for his guidance through the maze of publishing.

Finally, as an entrepreneur, I have been blessed with a business partner, Al Rhodes, who has become my best friend and a dependable hardworking partner. Together, we have built a fantastic business, overcome major obstacles, and maintained a meaningful friendship along the way. In today's business world, this is rare and difficult to achieve. Business partnerships are notorious for the challenges they present. Al's incredible intelligence, perseverance, and quiet, confident demeanor have been a blessing to me and to our business. And most valuable to me is the respect and support he has shown me as I have explored my academic and writing interests.

Many thanks to you all.